D0295986

Floyd's
China

Floyd's
China

Keith Floyd

To Tess Floyd,
and my ever-patient editor Barbara Dixon

Special thanks to Pakistan International Airways and Captain Mian Naveed and his crew; the management and staff of the Crowne Plaza Hotel, Beijing; Katharina Hesse for the photographs.

Special thanks to my friend Mr Jing.

First published in 2005 by Collins
an imprint of
HarperCollins Publishers
77–85 Fulham Palace Road
London W6 8JB

www.collins.co.uk

Text © Keith Floyd 2005
Location photographs © Stan Green Management 2005
Food photographs (see below) © HarperCollins Publishers 2005

Keith Floyd reserves the moral right to be identified as the author of the Work.

Keith Floyd is represented by Stan Green Management, Dartmouth, Devon; telephone 01803 770046; fax 01803 770075; e-mail TV@stangreen.co.uk Visit www.keithfloyd.co.uk

All rights reserved. No part of this publication may be reproduced, stored in a retrieval system, or transmitted, in any form or by any means, electronic, mechanical, photocopying, recording or otherwise, without the prior written permission of the publishers.

A catalogue record for this book is available from the British Library

Book produced for Collins by Essential Works Ltd
Editor: Barbara Dixon
Designer: Mark Stevens
Location photographer: Katharina Hesse
Photographs page 8 (bottom): Adrian Worsley, Production Manager
Studio food photographer: Michelle Garrett
Home Economist: Carole Handslip
Indexer: Hazel Bell
Cover photographs: Katharina Hesse

Food photographs: (a = above, b = below, l = left, r = right, c = centre, t = top)
1c; 34 bl; 35 bl; 36 c, r; 44; 45; 50 tr; 55; 56; 57; 68 t; 70 c; 72, 74; 78; 79; 89 tl, br; 90; 94; 95; 104 br; 105 br; 106 tl; 114; 115; 137 tl, br; 141; 145; 146; 148; 149; 155; 156 tr, br; 157 cl, cr, br; 159; 164; 166–9; 173; 174 tl, bl, cr; 175 tl, br; 176 l, c; 179; 181; 183–4; 186; 188–9

ISBN 0–00–714657–4

Colour reproduction by CPI Bath

Printed and bound by Butler and Tanner, Frome, Somerset, UK

Contents

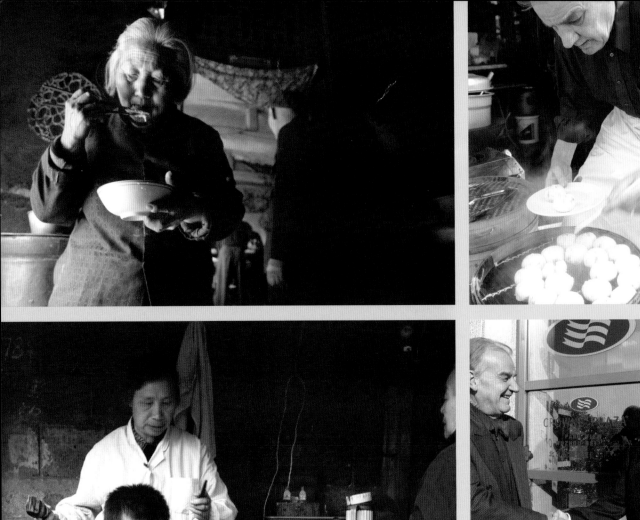

Introduction

Introduction

Next stop China!

It is a long haul from Heathrow to Beijing via Islamabad! And if you fly Pakistan International Airways, as I did, it is a very long, dry haul. There is, after all, only so much fruit juice you can drink and, of course, in common with all other airlines, you cannot smoke either, although I noticed, while I was on the flight deck with Captain Mian Naveed, his pipe was close at hand. I passed a couple of happy hours with him, a most amusing and philosophical gentleman.

I returned to my seat for dinner, served from a rickety old trolley, with wonderful dishes of Pakistani food – dhal, lamb korma, saffron rice, spinach and cottage cheese, delicious food – and when the steward noticed that I had, in fact, eaten everything including the bits of raw chilli in some of the dishes he said, 'You like Pakistani food?', 'Yup', I said, 'I sure do.' 'Would you like some more?' he said. 'You bet,' I said, and had second helpings. Instead of my usual alcoholic digestif to follow, I had a refreshing cup of green tea.
Beijing, here I come!

Wow! What a swept-up airport there is in Beijing. Six o'clock in the morning and silence. Tick the boxes in my health immigration card. Pad gently through the long marble-floored corridors and climb gratefully into the limousine to take me to my hotel.

Below left to right *On the flight deck with the friendly crew from Pakistan International Airways; tucking into my dinner on board; signing in at the Crowne Plaza Hotel, Beijing.* Opposite *Could this be the Great Wall?*

Opposite top to bottom *'Baozis' (Chinese steamed buns) in a bakery outside the White Cloud Taoist Temple, Beijing; the hotel kitchen.*
Above *Helping the Executive Chef of the Crowne Plaza Hotel.*

At the Crowne Plaza there is a reception committee. The general manager, the executive chef and several European acolytes are waiting to show me to my room. But, I don't want to go to my room. I want some breakfast! And, by the way, I would quite like a drink of the non-fruit juice kind.

In the dining room's kitchen, behind the long counters, there is the smiling face of a chubby head chef and, further along, serene ladies are wrapping up dim sums, but what I want is congee. They have four different varieties of congee for breakfast. But for those of you who don't know what congee is, it is basically a porridge made from rice. Rice cooked in chicken stock. As simple as that, but by the time you have added pickled ginger, chillies, a couple of cooked prawns or some shredded chicken, you have a breakfast that can blast you into the stratosphere. After two bowls of congee, I returned to the buffet and my big, fat, smiling Chinese cook said, 'What would you like next?' So, I chose some spicy chicken with black beans and a plate of freshly boiled noodles garnished with crispy deep-fried onions, some ginger and pickled cucumber. When I say pickled cucumber, this is simply cucumber that has been marinated in rice vinegar. I helped myself to a large spoon of fresh chilli sauce – again very simple, chillies chopped up in oil. I was beginning to feel better after my nearly 48-hour journey (because I had overnighted in Islamabad), so I returned again to the buffet and got myself a plate of stir-fried pak choi, melon, green peppers and ginger. It was 7.30 a.m. but I noticed there was a Japanese section at the other end of this wonderful open kitchen, so I had a couple of bowls of clear chicken broth and some raw tuna fish with wasabi and pickled ginger. It was now 8.30 a.m. and, whereas time and tide wait for no man, it was time for a kip.

I took the lift to my room, switched on the television and, to my horror, Star Asia was showing *Floyd on Fish*, a programme I had made over 20 years ago. I opened the mini bar, selected a stiff one and went to sleep.

Refreshed, showered and altogether more up together, I discovered it was lunchtime. My chubby Chinese cook was still there, smiling, happy, and remembered me from breakfast. He had a crispy roast duck and carved it neatly for me, suggesting I take some steamed rice and pickles. And then, to my delight, when I wandered up to the bit where they have the puddings, there was a pot or dish of baked apple custard. Now, this surprised me, because I felt, or I thought I knew, the Chinese had no particular lactic cuisine, but was it good! And next to that were some very simple apple fritters sprinkled with cinnamon. God, I was feeling better!

Below The excellent Mr Jing and his little red taxi – Great Wall, here we come.

Above *After that climb I needed a little support.*

My assistant, who comes unashamedly from Cumbria, chose the European option for lunch. Why do people travel thousands of miles to eat lasagne and chips that the Old Bull and Bush serves every lunchtime? I just got myself a few more fritters and waited to meet my photographer, who turned out to be an elegant, tall, Chinese-speaking German who had fallen in love with China many years before and now based her life and career in the People's Republic. She said she wanted to be called Kat. She was probably 30 and had proposed that our first shoot should be on the Great Wall of China. So, the following morning at 5.00 a.m. we set off in a little red car driven by Mr Jing to the Great Wall at Mutianyu. This particular entrance to the Great Wall is the most grotesque tourist-orientated place you can imagine. People hollering, T-shirts for sale, worse than Brighton Pier; and even after you have taken the cable car up to the first level, you still have the steps to climb, created presumably by some Mongolian or Chinese emperor, which are each about three feet high. I find myself having to climb the final steps on my hands and knees, I could not do it, and yet the Saga louts with their walking sticks and rucksacks were springing up like newborn monkeys. Believe you me, if anyone says 'take a trip to the Great Wall' don't bother. It is reconstructed, of course, it is magnificent, but when you get knocked over by hoardes of Swedes, Americans, Germans, Japanese, etc., all clutching their T-shirts, the mystique somehow disappears. The only sane man

Above *A view of the landscape near the Great Wall in Mutianyu on the outskirts of Beijing.* Opposite *Lemon slices and flower buds are sold as tea in a street market in Beijing.*

that day was Mr Jing, who, when we arrived at the barrier of the car park, which would have forced me to have walked another 200 metres, refused to be kowtowed and said, 'I am taking Mr Floyd to the closest point possible!' If you ever find yourself in Beijing (once know as, Peking and before that Ping Pong), call up Mr Jing. Without Mr Jing, life would be as for Bertie Wooster without Jeeves!

The morning had been cold, but now it was hot and overcast and in the hot wind it was snowing little puffballs of blossom as we bounced along in Mr Jing's uncomfortable, hot, cramped car, smoking Mr Jing's Chinese cigarettes. It had taken us three hours to get to the Great Wall instead of the estimated one hour. Jet lag and the early morning start were weighing heavily upon me as we headed back to Beijing. Mr Jing, with his trousers rolled up to his knees, was chattering away and, from time to time, poured some warm tea from a screw-top jam jar and handed it to me. Apparently all Beijing drivers carry endless quantities of tea in their cars and also endless packets of cigarettes, but then tea drinking is a cult in China. There are three kinds: fermented (red/black), unfermented (green) and semi-fermented (Oolong). Then there are the smoked teas, the scented teas and chrysanthemum tea. The flavours can vary enormously depending on which province the tea has been grown in and each has its own subtle fragrance. Tea is drunk all day and is considered good for just about anything that ails you; and by the way, it's also still sold in bricks in China. But I digress. Anyway, we pulled over to the side of the road where there was a stall selling nuts and fruits and we were greeted, to my surprise, by a diminutive, elderly lady in a brightly coloured frock who led us across the road, chattering comfortably with Mr Jing and with

the photographer, and into her one-storey, brick-built, shabby little bungalow. The garden had a rudimentary chicken coop and there were stacks of dried maize stalks, piles of nappa cabbage and a few tomatoes, but it was neglected and somehow rather sad. We went into the cool, gloomy house, illuminated by two flickering lightbulbs without shades, one in the kitchen and one in the other room. To the left and right of the kitchen door were two stone-built rectangles, each one containing an iron built-in dish about three feet in diameter. These were wood-fired, or maize stalk-fired, woks, that indispensable cooking utensil in China. We went into the other room, which had two chairs, a large built-in wooden bed about eight feet long, a bucket of water, a small table and shabby walls covered with garish photographs of Chairman Mao. Mrs Li's husband (Mr Yang) sat, serene but smiling in his blue overalls. He was probably seventy. I didn't know what was going on and I know not to ask. When something good happens, let it happen. There were three or four ladies in the cramped room and in a battered aluminium bowl they mixed flour and water into a dough, rolled it out very thinly and then cut it deftly into circles about three inches in diameter. Meanwhile, the old man, bent, slowly collected maize stalks from the garden and lit a fire under one of the huge woks. While he did this, the ladies chopped wild, green vegetables for which I have no translation – perhaps wild spinach or lovage, and other herbs; they added a little rice vinegar to this mixture and deftly, so deftly, rolled them into balls the size of a marble, folded them into the little rounds of dough and formed them into crescent shapes. After the smoke had settled, the water in the wok began to boil and one by one they dropped these

Opposite top to bottom *Mrs Li stands next to the fireplace in her farmhouse; Mr Yang puts wood into the fire under the wok.* **Below left to right** *Mrs Li fries wild herbs; Mrs Sun (l) and a neighbour arrange dumplings on a plate before they are cooked; Mr Yang looks on.*

Above left to right *A vendor flies a magnificent kite; the horrendous traffic in Beijing; at Din Tai Fung restaurant, a waiter picks up freshly made dim sum from the kitchen.* Opposite *Excellent dim sum at Din Tai Fung.*

wonderful dumplings into the water. After ten or fifteen minutes they were cooked and we all sat upon this built-in bed with a narrow plank of wood on stubby legs between us and ate these amazing dumplings.

They showed me the crude cellar in the garden, where, in former times, they had kept their cabbages and potatoes for use during the winter. They made green tea, talked and smiled and urged me to eat more. They had no money, barely any kind of a pension, but they had a dignity and a kindness that was most moving. Outside on the sill of the window, which in common with houses built at that time had no glass, just a kind of paper tissue, there lay drying in the sun a pile of orange peel, crisp like a poppadom, which they infused in boiling water and used as a remedy for colds, tummy upsets and as a general cure-all.

We shook hands, we hugged and said goodbye and bounced off down the congested road back to town, but again Mr Jing stopped, this time at a place the size of a European garden centre, next to a large plot of exquisite pottery – dragons, urns, pots, fish, warriors. There was nothing growing on the floor of the place that brought to mind a garden centre, but the sky was fluttering, clacking, flicking and swooping with hundreds of magnificent kites. They were purple, vermillion, orange, ochre, green, and red and on the ground there were row upon row of these multi-coloured kites in the shapes of hawks, eagles, fish and dragons. I bought two kites, each one with a wingspan of about eight feet, and Mr Jing made the staff fly them for me to see that they were right. They reeled them in on a large hand-held fishing reel and Mr Jing handled the transaction and, my God, he drives a hard bargain. These two exquisite flying creatures, because creatures they are, cost me the princely sum of three pounds! They are fragile and fine and I managed to get them back to France, undamaged and unbroken.

We made good progress towards Beijing until we hit the city. The traffic is horrendous, on four- or five-laned highways that cross the city of multi-storey buildings. Gotham City. Finally, we made it to a quiet parking lot and into an elegant, minimalist, glass-fronted restaurant called Din Tai Fung, allegedly Beijing's finest dim sum restaurant. Dim sums, both sweet and savoury, were in former times served in tea houses so that businessmen, artists, philosophers and poets could sip tea and have a light snack while they discussed the day's affairs. I suppose it was the Chinese version of an early English coffee house or a proper French café. The kitchen was screened by glass and you could see the sixteen or seventeen cooks working deftly, but it was surreal. I had hoped to enter the kitchen myself to observe very closely what they were doing, but I was not granted permission. They were clad in immaculate white uniforms, white, ankle-length rubber boots, thin, white rubber gloves, crisp paper hats and masks. The fear of SARS still lingers. We ate some dim sum, drank some tea, took as many pictures as time would allow and worked out the recipes as best we could – many Chinese are very reluctant to reveal their culinary secrets to you. However, that did not stop me from finding out because I had Mr Jing.

By 9.30 p.m. I was back at the hotel, tired, elated, exhilarated and anxious for an early night. We had after all started at 5.00 a.m., but unfortunately, as I walked into the, if you like, Chinese brasserie of the hotel I was recognized and hijacked by a multi-national team that was there sponsoring the Johnny Walker Golf Tournament. Later I had some steamed sea bass with ginger, some plain boiled rice and a bowl of fresh fruit and then happily took the lift to my room on the fifth floor. I lay on the bed and continued to read Patrick O'Brian's *Desolation Island* and minutes later the phone rang and it was 5.00 a.m. again!

I had read in the hotel's brochure that a good way to enjoy Beijing would be to hire a bicycle and ride around: that must have been written in about 1954. It is utter bollocks, there is no way you can safely ride around the congested streets of this city. But, I had some lamb curry and some noodles, just quickly boiled with fresh greens thrown in, and set off anyway around the streets looking for what people ate for breakfast. Everybody seems to eat steamed buns, a bit like a dumpling with a little tiny bit of slightly sweet meat inside, or a deep-fried 'youtiao', a sort of long doughnut made from rice flour and water that costs ha'pennies. Others would go into little restaurants and have a bowl of noodles or a bowl of soup.

Below left to right *Once I took to the road, all the cars disappeared; 'Youtiao' translates as 'oily stick' and are part of the traditional Northern Chinese breakfast; I enjoyed this one in Beijing's Tuanjiehu District.*

Above left to right *A migrant from Hubei province spreads dough to make a Shandong-style pancake; folding the pancake; Mr Jing looks envious as I enjoy my pancake in a market near Julong Gardens.*

I chanced upon one really amazing street vendor. He had a large circular plancha, about two and a half feet in diameter, which was mounted above a charcoal fire on a spindle so he could spin this wheel around. He would spin it, pour a ladleful of his maize flour pancake mix onto it and all the while the wheel was turning he would scrape it out and scrape it out until he had a thin disk of a pancake about two feet in diameter. He flipped it over to his wife who filled it with finely chopped salad, coriander and chillies and folded it into a manageable envelope. It was outstanding.

On we went to the central market: sacks of chillies, dried fungus, dried mushrooms, mountains of Chinese greens, tank upon tank of live fish, frogs, snakes, turtles, mountains of pigs' ears, pigs' trotters, pigs' intestines, pigs' hearts, fat, plump ducks, chickens, chicken feet, chicken necks, chicken wings, pigs' tails, ox tails, beef tripe, pork chitterlings, hearts, kidneys, lights. For me it was better than the finest art gallery, but I am sure many from the West would have found it unacceptable.

Then the fish section. Mountains of oysters, clams, snails, winkles, sea slugs, sea urchins. It was hot, the floor was awash in water, trampled leaves and crushed entrails. The pervading smell was slightly stomach turning, a long way from the clinical aisles of a Western supermarket. But I loved it. And I managed to buy my tinned, coppered steamboat, a sort of a charcoal-fired fondue set in which you heat stock and cook shrimps and vermicelli noodles, prawns and thin slivers of beef or chicken, greens and mushrooms.

It went on like this relentlessly for days as I left Beijing and toured the surrounding countryside. I cooked in kitchens and made stir-frys over the blasting fire of their cookers, which could propel a 747 into the stratosphere. These cookers are, of course, the secret of Chinese cookery. They are so powerful

that everything cooks extremely quickly, literally in seconds, and you have to be sharp, you have to be swift and stay completely calm in this volcanic, gastronomic atmosphere. Whoever said the Americans invented fast food? Their version may be fast but it ain't what I call food.

Of course, in some of the kitchens that they smilingly, and laughingly, let me into, I just couldn't cope. I couldn't roll out a four-foot rectangle of noodle dough then throw it up into the air, rather like a man clapping hands, and turn it within seconds into millimetre-thin lengths of noodle. That is an art, but an art that is taken for granted.

Back in Beijing I had to go to Tiananmen Square, I had to go to the Forbidden City, but I'm sorry, I am a cook, not a tourist, and Tiananmen Square may be the biggest in the world, but I am afraid I was very disappointed to discover it is just a square. No jugglers, no dragons, no clowns and no street food hawkers, just a man in sandals, jeans and a T-shirt who tried to arrest me as I attempted to have my picture taken with one of the guards. Despite its outrageous opulence and the massive building project and the obsessive preparations for the Olympics in 2008 and despite the utterly charming nature of the Chinese people, you cannot help feeling the sinister undertones of an authoritarian regime. Yeah, I looked at a few temples and went to the weird night food market – hundreds of stalls, all of them red and white, all of them staffed by proprietors all dressed in red and white as if they worked for Kentucky Fried Chicken. The array of food was a little different, however. Grilled snakes, crispy snakeskin, deep-fried locusts or some other large insect, all kinds of

Opposite *Selecting my steamboat in the central market with the help of Mr Jing.* Below left to right *Frogs and snake skin are sold in Wangfujing night market; glutinous rice desserts are also sold there; in Tiananmen Square – the sun shines on the righteous.*

intestines alongside nice kebabs and vegetables, but I bailed out of that and went to Steamboat Street. Well, I called it Steamboat Street because all the restaurants there have steamboats. Not like the handmade steamboat I bought to impress my friends back in Europe, but here the steamboat, which is a metal bowl, is set into the table that you sit at, with a gas burner underneath it. They bring you a menu with a list of probably a thousand vegetables, meats, mushrooms, insects, fish, frogs, everything you can possibly imagine, or not imagine. All kinds of vermicelli, egg noodles, rice noodles. They pour some either mild or hot, depending on your taste, stock into the bowl, set fire to the gas and you just drop a few bits of food at a time into the stock, fish them out with a little wire basket and have an outstanding feast. The beef they bring you is sliced as thin as

Below *A delicate wonton soup (huntun) for breakfast.* Opposite top to bottom *Tucking into my hotpot at the Little Winter hotpot restaurant, Ghost Street; ever get the feeling you're being watched?*

the thinnest Parma ham, so, of course, all these things cook in seconds, but you can take hours to eat it. Take good friends with you. My assistant from Cumbria, may God long preserve him, was again really thinking about a nice lasagne and chips and somehow failed to share my enthusiasm.

If Beijing has an equivalent of Langan's Brasserie, Simpson's in the Strand, The Ivy or the Rib Room at the Carlton Towers, then it has to be a restaurant called Old Beijing Zhajiang Noodle King at 29 Chong Wai Street, Chong Wen District, Beijing. There is one difference, however, and it is a big one. This stylish, long-established, noisy, clattering, garrulous rendezvous of the Gucci-shoed, Rolex-wearing, mobile phone-chattering, finely dressed Chinese ladies and gentlemen, serves only noodles. They bring you a bowl of noodles and you choose one of about 400 things to put on top of it. It is sensational. It is friendly and it is professional and it won't f*** up your credit card! Also, if like me you love a roasted, free-range, Gressingham duck with giblet gravy and apple sauce, or, if like me you are nostalgic enough and romantic enough to think that the Tour d'Argent in Paris serves the best duck, then you must visit the Imperial Duck Trading Corporation – actually, that is not its name, it is, in fact, called Quanjaid. It's on the second or third floor of one of these imposing skyscrapers, it has been in operation since about 1850 and it specialises, of course, in Peking Duck. These specially reared and fattened ducks are air-dried for two days before they are roasted vertically in front of a wood-fired oven so that the skin is crisp and almost opaque, like golden glass. The duck is served to you with its head on, the skin is deftly carved off and given to you separately, and then comes the unctuous meat, the little pancakes, the plum sauce, the strips of spring onions and cucumber, which you roll and munch, meanwhile sipping a creamy duck broth, and finally the waiter comes back and carves the long duck tongue into fine slivers for you. But he too looked like someone from Mars because he was wearing a white suit, white boots, white gloves and a mask. As you leave you notice all the signed photographs on the wall from Nixon to Chairman Mao and beyond.

Thank you, China. I will be back.

Keith Floyd
Uzes
South East France
June 2005

Opposite top to bottom *A treat in store at Old Beijing Zhajiang Noodle King; Mr Jing finds my company hilarious.*

Kissing don't last, cooking do

Confucious said, 'Give a man a fish and he will live for a day. Teach a man to fish and he will live forever.' He also said, although he, of course, said a lot of things, 'Eating is the utmost important part of life.' I don't have to hand any of his quotations on the art of lovemaking.

The celebrated food writer and gastronaught, although I fear she would disapprove of that term, Jane Grigson, who, along with Elizabeth David, was one of the best food writers in the English language, said that cooking is a very simple art, you apply heat to raw food and keep it as simple as possible.

In Britain we are blessed with a multicultural, culinary society and can enjoy the world's food cooked by Thais, Italians, French, Spanish, Indians and, of course, the likes of home-grown British talent such as Gary Rhodes, Gordon Ramsay, Antony Worrall Thompson, et al. There is not a town in the land that does not have a Chinese takeaway. It is popular food and invariably it is often not very good. It is so Westernized – that is to say it does not have the 'umph' of real Eastern cooking and it has actually become a bit of a joke. Stir-fried bean sprouts with a bit of chicken and no real seasoning, no real spice, no real passion behind it is quite frankly a disaster. However, there are good restaurants around in places like Manchester, Soho and, indeed, in Brighton, where the excellent China Garden serves unctuous, sticky rice in lotus leaves and curried whelks, which are as good as anything you can find anywhere in the world, although I do acknowledge that Hong Kong and Taiwan are pretty good too! In Hong Kong there is a restaurant that serves dim sum – it seats 1,000 people and the waiters and waitresses endlessly push trollies to your table with delectable compositions, be it prawns, pork, chicken, frog's legs, sea snakes, sea cucumbers, or whatever. Brilliant dumplings, excellent concoctions of noodles.

So what then is Chinese food? It is not a little box of quickly fried red and green peppers, a bit of beef and black bean sauce purchased after 10 pints of lager at 11.00 at night. Chinese food is the result of thousands of years of civilization. The vast country of China has suffered from poor harvests and during those lean years, to stay alive, the Chinese would explore anything edible. As a consequence, many wonderful and slightly incredible ingredients, such as lily buds, wood ears, vegetable peels and shark's fins, were incorporated into the exquisite richness and variety of Chinese food. You may not want to eat sea cucumbers (a kind of a slug), you may not want a piece of grilled snakeskin or a brochette of strange insects. I think I don't either, but the sheer volume and variety of food is gastronomically mind boggling – particularly, for me, the noodles. There are so many – egg noodles, wheat noodles, rice flour noodles. Wheat noodles are common in Shanghai. These are thick and when cooked and

Above left to right *Minced meat and onions being fried for the dumpling filling at Mrs Li's house; stuffed pancakes are fried in a wok at a mountain restaurant; bakers prepare baozi in a bakery outside the White Cloud Taoist Temple, Beijing.*

stir-fried with a savoury sauce of chicken, pork or shrimp are delicious. Rice flour noodles, often known as Singapore style, use thin, vermicelli noodles seasoned with curry powder and mixed with shrimp or barbequed pork or ham.

Basically there are two types of noodle dish. One is a plate of boiled noodles with pork or duck and some vegetables and accompanied with a cup of soup; the other, what we know as chow mein, are pan- or wok-fried noodles mixed with stir-fried meat, vegetables or seafood. But, most importantly, and this is why it is hard to really re-create Chinese food in a Western kitchen, especially if you happen to have a halogen hob electric cooker, the Chinese cookers and the woks that sit on them have such intense, instant, volcanic heat that things can be cooked very quickly, thus maintaining the flavours, vitamins and the healthiness of this food. If you enjoy stir-frying dishes, for an authentic flavour you may well be advised to buy a powerful camping gaz-type stove, a bottle of gas and cook it outside.

The Chinese love food – love buying it, discussing it and love to eat communally, whether at home or in a restaurant. Not for them a table for two – large round tables for 10, 15 or 20 are quite common. They also mostly use fresh ingredients, which can mean two trips a day to the market. And nothing is wasted – you name it, the Chinese will find a way to cook it, be it chicken's feet, jellyfish or sea slugs. Not to mention the grilled insects, bird, frogs and snakes.

The cuisine is built around the five tastes: sweet, sour, bitter, pungent and salty, and on the techniques of steaming, braising, stir-frying, deep-frying, boiling and roasting. Fermentation is also used to produce sauces such as soy sauce – that quintessentially Chinese seasoning – and pickled ginger, salted black beans, and many more. Add to the equation a grain food – usually boiled or steamed rice – and you have the foundation for your Chinese meal.

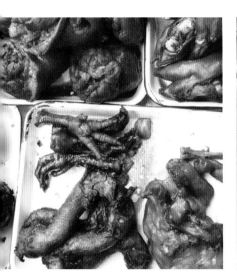

Above left to right *Pigs' feet, ducks' feet and duck throats for sale in the market; cooks at Din Tai Fung prepare dim sum; at the Hakka restaurant in Chaoyang District they kindly allowed me to cook. Hakka food is that of the Han people.*

Not surprisingly in a country as vast as China, there are four distinct regions, each with its own cooking style – northern/Peking; western/Sichuan; Eastern/Shanghai; and southern/Canton.

Back here, we have our Peking, Cantonese and Sichuan restaurants. Very broadly speaking, we have only to add Shanghai cuisine and we have the four gastronomic regions of China, each with its own peculiarities.

I started my journey in Beijing, or Peking as it was known, and Peking cuisine is that of the north. The main staple here is wheat – steamed bread and noodles are the most common produce, as well as the popular breakfast street food 'youtiao', mentioned earlier. An equally popular dish in the north is dumplings, stuffed with a variety of fillings, and eaten with a vinegar dip, soy sauce or what you fancy. The most famous dish has to be Peking Duck, so called because it was originally made with the special ducks bred near Peking. Other specialities of the north include chestnuts, Chinese cabbage, seafood (in Shandong province), offal and noodles, while the Chinese Muslims of the area are lovers of lamb and beef – the Mongolian beef hotpot on page 94 is a particular favourite. Oh yes, and they brew a very good beer called Tsingtao – great with dumplings!

To the east we find Shanghai cuisine. A land of lakes, canals and rivers, the region is abundant in both fresh- and seawater fish, as well as rice, wheat and corn. It's where they make the famous Shaoxing (Shaohsing) rice wine, and wine features in many dishes of the area, as does oil, fat and sugar, giving the cuisine a style of its own. Red-braised dishes are a well-known speciality, as are stir-fried eel and crab, shrimp, prawn and fish dishes.

Cantonese, or southern cuisine, is the most versatile of the four, as well as the lightest – less oil, sugar, garlic, chilli and seasoning are used than in the other cuisines. But what it lacks in strong flavours, it makes up for in subtleness of flavour and texture – crisp is very crispy, smooth is very smooth. Stir-frying excels here, and we have this region to thank for dim sum – that vast variety of Chinese 'hors d'oeuvres' enjoyed at breakfast and lunch. Each area throughout this region has its own specialities, be it chicken, tripe, mustard greens, seafood or soups, but given their sub-tropical climate, they all enjoy a wide variety of tropical fruits, the lychee being the most abundant. And by the way, if you like snake, this is the place to come to eat it.

Lastly, we have Sichuan, or western cuisine, whose food is mainly hot and spicy. Sichuan peppercorns and red chillies are used extensively to add intensity to the dishes, as are garlic, ginger and salt. The west is a landlocked area and to compensate for the lack of fresh fish, a fermented fish sauce is added to many dishes, which also feature a variety of shapes and tastes. Here is to be found more varieties of edible fungi than in any other province of China. It's also the home of Maotai wine – not a wine, in fact, but a potent distilled spirit. And believe you me, Maotai wine is terrifying! Take it from one who has dedicated his life to food, drink and the enjoyment of cooking, go easy on that one. You have been warned.

And finally (excluding the Japanese), the joy of cooking Chinese food is that you can take pleasure in cutting your vegetables, your squid or your scallops into artistic and mouthwatering shapes. But most importantly, and again I emphasize, you need a lot of heat, the ingredients cut into small pieces and then cooked quickly. Fast food, fine food.

Below left to right *Sugar-coated fruit and corn are sold in the Wangfujing night market; adding prawns to my hotpot at the Little Winter hotpot restaurant, Ghost Street; back at base with the cooks in the hotel.*

Quantities

The delight of Chinese food is that you don't have to measure it precisely. Since the essence of Chinese food is sharing, one dish of noodles in this book, for example, will be served between four and six people. So, to enjoy a really good Chinese lunch or dinner party using these recipes – which I have selected because I love them – make two, three or four different dishes and share them with your friends.

In Chinese cooking you just cannot say, for example, that one 1.35 kg/3 lb chicken roasted will serve four people. Because the Chinese, whether they are mixing fish, vegetables or meat with either noodles or rice, will stretch it to suit the occasion. After all, most Chinese cooks don't weigh, measure or time – they are intuitive and instinctive cooks, they don't buy cookery books, they don't watch television cookery programmes and they will never, ever have heard of *Ready Steady Cook*, *Hell's Kitchen* or anything else of that ilk.

Below *These chaps are masters of their art;* Opposite top to bottom *A grocery store in Yongning District; hotpot.*

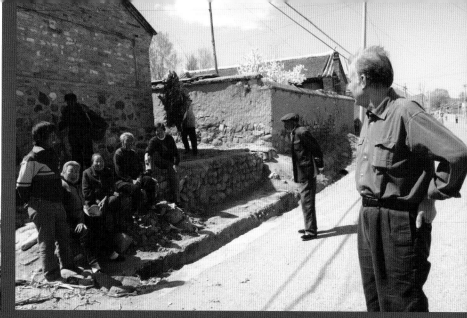
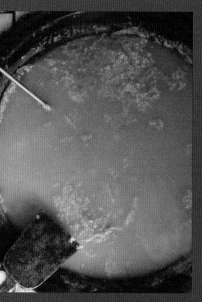

Soup

Above left to right *A lantern in an old alley in Houhai District; bamboo shoot and meatball soup (page 44); red chillies.*

Soup

Chinese soups can be served at any stage of the meal.

Although the soups are often thin and watery, those included

here are more substantial and you could eat them as a meal on

their own, for lunch.

All these soups can be garnished with thin slivers of fried

garlic (see page 185), tiny pieces of crisply fried shallot,

chopped coriander, mint, chives, parsley or basil,

matchstick-sized batons of cucumber and finely chopped

green or red chillies.

Above *A cook cleans and cuts mushrooms for lunch outside a restaurant near Beihai Park in Beijing.*

These little garnishes can be prepared in advance and then placed in bowls on the table so that the diners can help themselves to their taste.

Diners can also add more soy sauce, chilli sauce or indeed a dash of oyster sauce, if liked.

Above *This vendor proudly introduced me to her son in a street market in Beijing.* Opposite *Kitchen utensils neatly placed, at a farmhouse in a village outside Beijing.*

Duck and cabbage soup

1 small plump duck with giblets
3 thin slices peeled fresh root ginger,
   finely chopped
450 g / 1 lb dark green-leaved bok choi
sea salt and freshly ground black pepper

1 Preheat the oven to 200°C/400°F/gas mark 6. Prick the breast of the duck with the point of a sharp knife and rub well with salt. Place on a trivet in a roasting tray with a little water and roast breast side down for 30 minutes. Reduce the heat to 180°C/350°F/gas mark 4, turn the bird over onto its back and roast for a further 60 minutes. When the duck is cooked, take it out of the oven and leave to cool completely, then carve all the flesh from the carcase and put to one side.

2 Break up the carcase and place in a large pan with the giblets and roasting juices, cover with water, add the ginger and bring to the boil. Reduce the heat to very low and simmer, uncovered, for about 40 minutes.

3 Remove the carcase and giblets and skim off any fat that has risen to the surface of the broth.

4 Chop the white stem of the bok choi into thin slices and rip up the green leaves into coarse pieces. Add the bok choi and the duck meat to the broth, heat gently to warm through, then season to taste and serve.

Thick spicy and sour soup

1.5 litres / 2½ pints chicken stock
2.5 cm / 1 inch piece black pudding, cut into strips
25 g / 1 oz cooked, skinned duck breast, shredded
1 block of tofu or bean curd, shredded
6 or 7 oyster mushrooms, or straw mushrooms, cut into strips
25 g / 1 oz shredded bamboo shoots
1 red chilli, deseeded and chopped
3 spring onions, trimmed and chopped
1 tablespoon white rice vinegar or white wine vinegar
1 teaspoon crushed black peppercorns
1 dessertspoon cornflour mixed with a little cold water to the consistency of single cream
1 egg, beaten
1 tablespoon chilli oil, to finish

1 Heat the stock in a pan and add all the ingredients except the cornflour mixture, beaten egg and chilli oil.

2 Bring to the boil, then reduce the heat and simmer for about 5 minutes.

3 Pour in the cornflour mixture and stir until the soup has thickened.

4 Whisk in the beaten egg until it is distributed around the soup and set, then pour the soup into individual bowls, sprinkle with a little chilli oil and serve.

Pork and tomato soup

100 g / 3½ oz very thinly sliced lean pork, cut into strips
2 teaspoons dry sherry, sake or rice wine
2 teaspoons light soy sauce
1 onion, peeled and finely chopped
3 tomatoes, deseeded and chopped
1.5 litres / 2½ pints chicken stock
1 egg, beaten
vegetable oil, for stir-frying
sea salt and freshly ground black pepper
freshly chopped coriander leaves, to garnish

1 Put the pork in a bowl with the sherry, sake or rice wine and the soy sauce and leave to marinate for 30 minutes.

2 Heat the oil in a pan, add the onion and the pork mixture and stir-fry for a couple of minutes, to brown lightly.

3 Add the tomatoes and stock and bring to the boil, then season with salt and pepper, reduce the heat and simmer gently for about 5 minutes.

4 Add the beaten egg and stir until the egg is just setting, then serve immediately, garnished with the coriander.

Opposite *At work cutting tofu in the kitchen of the excellent Hakka restaurant, Chaoyang District.*

Above *An elderly man sells dried fruits and herbs near the Great Wall at Mutianyu.*

Chicken and ginseng soup

1 litre/1¾ pints chicken stock
3.5 cm/1½ inches ginseng root, sliced
1 handful of sultanas
1 cm/½ inch piece fresh root ginger,
   peeled and finely sliced
2 skinless, boneless chicken breasts,
   sliced into strips
2 shallots, peeled and finely sliced
vegetable oil, for frying
sea salt, to taste

1 Bring the stock to the boil in a pan, add the ginseng, sultanas and ginger, then reduce the heat and simmer gently for about 30 minutes.

2 Add the chicken and simmer for a further 10 minutes.

3 While the soup is simmering, heat a pan or wok, add a little oil and stir-fry the shallots until they are golden brown and crispy. Remove from the pan and drain on kitchen paper.

4 Season the soup with salt, pour into individual bowls and garnish with the crispy shallots.

Fragrant soup with spinach and meatballs

for the meatballs

200 g / 7 oz lean pork

1 teaspoon preserved Sichuan mustard
(or you could use Dijon)

1 egg white

1 tsp sea salt

½ red or green chilli, deseeded

a small handful of coriander leaves

1 teaspoon cornflour

for the soup

1.5 litres / 2½ pints chicken stock

2 teaspoons light soy sauce

a splash of rice wine, sake or dry sherry

20 g / ¾ oz baby spinach leaves, washed
and dried

6 straw mushrooms, or chestnut or oyster
mushrooms, sliced

1 Place all the ingredients for the meatballs in a food processor and whiz until they are finely minced. Tip the mixture into a bowl and put in the fridge for about 20 minutes to cool and firm up a little.

2 When firmer to handle, roll the meat in your hands into little balls 1–1.5 cm / ½–¾ inch in diameter and put to one side.

3 To make the soup, pour the stock into a pan, add the soy sauce and rice wine, sake or sherry and bring to the boil.

4 Reduce the heat to a simmer, carefully drop in the meatballs and simmer for 3–4 minutes until the meatballs are cooked and floating on top of the broth.

5 Take off the heat and add the spinach leaves and mushrooms. Leave until they have just started to wilt, then serve.

Below left to right *This elderly gentleman was writing poems with a huge brush in an alley in Houhai District, Beijing.*

Bamboo shoot and meatball soup

for the meatballs

350 g / 12 oz slightly fatty pork, minced

3 spring onions, trimmed and very finely
    chopped

2.5 cm / 1 inch piece fresh root ginger,
    peeled and grated

1 teaspoon cornflour

freshly ground black pepper

for the soup

1 onion, peeled and chopped fairly finely

1 stringed celery stick, chopped fairly
    finely

1.5 litres / 2½ pints chicken stock

130 g can bamboo shoots, rinsed,
    drained and finely sliced

6 or 8 straw mushrooms, or chestnut or
    oyster mushrooms, sliced into strips

vegetable oil, for frying

sea salt

green leaves of spring onion, finely
    chopped, to garnish

1 Put all the ingredients for the meatballs in a bowl and mix thoroughly, then put into the fridge for about 30 minutes to firm up.

2 Using your hands, form the meatball mixture into small balls about the size of a marble.

3 To make the soup, heat a little oil in a pan and gently fry the onion and celery until they just begin to soften.

4 Add the stock, bamboo shoots and mushrooms and bring to a simmer, then gently drop in the meatballs and simmer for 7–10 minutes until the meatballs are poached. Season the soup with salt, pour into individual bowls, garnish with the spring onion and serve.

Thick mackerel and spinach soup

4 mackerel fillets, cut into 2.5 cm / 1 inch
  strips
a good handful of oyster mushrooms,
  sliced
1 medium carrot, peeled and cut into
  thin slivers
2 or 3 spring onions, trimmed and
  chopped
2.5 cm / 1 inch piece fresh root ginger,
  peeled and cut into fine strips
1.5 litres / 2½ pints fish stock
a dash of dry white wine
2 teaspoons cornflour mixed with a little
  cold water to the consistency of single
  cream
2 good handfuls of baby spinach leaves,
  washed and dried
a little vegetable oil, for stir-frying
sea salt and freshly ground black pepper
sesame oil, to finish

1 Heat the vegetable oil in a pan and stir-fry the mackerel until slightly crispy, then drain on kitchen paper.

2 Add the mushrooms, carrot, spring onions and ginger and stir-fry for a couple of minutes until just softening.

3 Pour in the stock and wine and bring to a simmer, then pour in the cornflour mixture and stir well until the soup starts to thicken.

4 Add the fish and spinach, season and remove from the heat. Pour over a few drops of sesame oil and serve hot.

Opposite *A vendor displays a bottle of Chinese cooking oil in a street market in Beijing.* **Below** *The fish section at Chaoyang wholesale market.*

Above *Three jolly chaps outside a shop in the market street at Yongning.* **Opposite** *This is the brunch area of the kitchen at the Crowne Plaza Hotel.*

Thick beef Chinese soup

250 g / 9 oz minced beef
1 teaspoon sea salt
1 teaspoon crushed black peppercorns
4 spring onions, trimmed and chopped
1 stringed celery stick, chopped
1 cm / ½ inch piece fresh root ginger, peeled and thinly sliced
1.5 litres / 2½ pints beef stock
a splash of rice wine, sake or dry sherry
2 teaspoons cornflour mixed with a little cold water to the consistency of single cream
1 small can sweetcorn, drained
4 egg whites
a little vegetable oil, for frying
a little sesame oil, to finish

1 Mix the minced beef with the salt and crushed peppercorns and put to one side.

2 Heat a little vegetable oil in a pan, add the spring onions, celery and ginger and stir-fry for a couple of minutes until they are soft but not coloured.

3 Add the stock and rice wine, sake or sherry and bring to the boil, then reduce the heat to a simmer, add the cornflour mixture and stir until slightly thickened.

4 Add the seasoned beef and stir slowly until the mince is distributed in the broth, then add the sweetcorn and simmer for about 10 minutes.

5 Add the egg white, stirring well until it is set, then pour the soup into individual bowls and serve with a little sesame oil sprinkled on top of each.

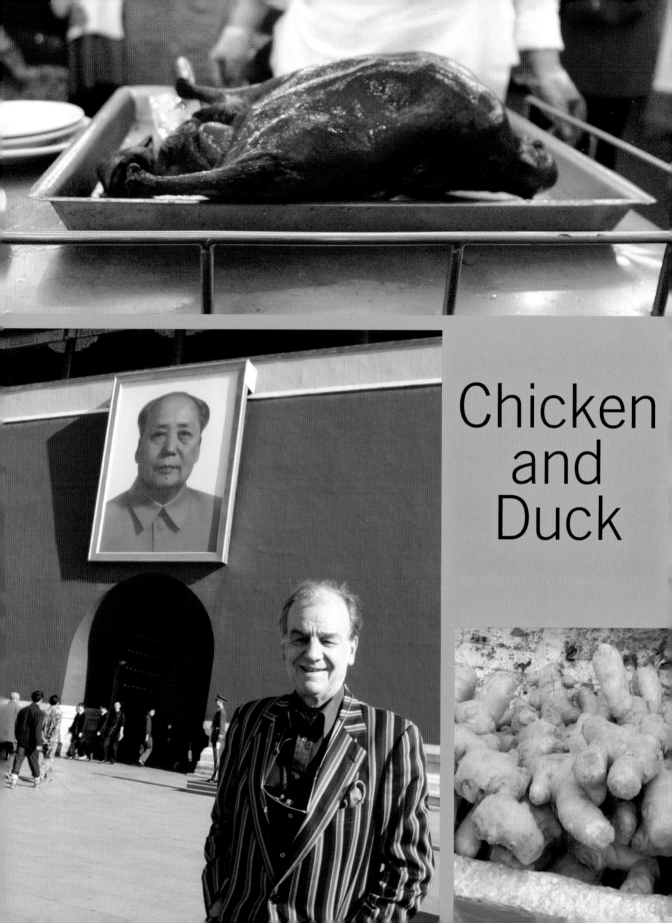

Chicken and Duck

Above *It was fascinating to watch this beekeeper at work in the countryside outside Beijing.*

Chicken and Duck

Despite its widespread availability, chicken is often a celebratory dish in China. However, unlike in the West, in China every bit of the bird is eaten, including the innards, neck and feet. The bird is cooked and served either whole or in pieces and either way it is not neatly dissected, but chopped up through the bone, using a large cleaver. The Chinese are expert in separating meat from bone in their mouths.

Duck is second in popularity to chicken and, of course, the most famous of the duck dishes has to be Peking Duck (see page 54), a labour of love, but worth every minute. In Beijing there are numerous restaurants specialising in this dish, including the excellent Quanjaid, where I enjoyed it.

Both chicken and duck can be combined with many vegetables and can be cooked in a number of ways. And, again, nothing is wasted – the feet, liver, giblets and even the blood are all put to use in one way and another.

Below *The mighty oven at one of the many duck restaurants in the city, the Li Qun.*

Roast duck, Peking style

This is one of the great dishes of China and notably served, in the home at least, at Chinese New Year with a specially reared, very plump duck. It would be ideal if you could obtain a seriously plump, free-range, non-frozen duck – a Gressingham duck, for example. I really would not bother using a frozen duck.

This dish is a labour of love, it takes two days to prepare, but my God it is worth it!

1 large plump duck, 1.5–1.75 kg/
   3½–4 lb in weight
300 ml / 10 fl oz water
2 heaped tablespoons soft brown sugar
1 teaspoon sea salt

for the filling
1 bunch of spring onions, trimmed, very
   top of the green leaves discarded but
   leaving 5–7.5 cm / 2–3 inches of green
   attached to the white part
½ cucumber, halved lengthways and
   deseeded
1 jar hoisin sauce

1 First morning – hang the duck by its neck in a cool airy place (a garden shed or wine cellar would be ideal!) and leave it there to dry for 24–30 hours.

2 Remove the head from the duck and prick the breast several times with the point of a very sharp knife.

3 Heat the water and dissolve the sugar and salt in it, then leave to cool. Paint the cooled sugar mixture liberally all over the duck and leave to dry. Paint it again, leave to dry and continue to do this until you have used up all the solution. Place the duck on a griddle and leave to dry once again. As all this will take 5–6 hours, you must start first thing in the morning.

4 While the duck is drying, we must address the accompaniments – cook the pancakes (see page 57) and prepare the filling.

5 Using a sharp knife, cut the green leaves of the spring onions in half lengthways, turn the onion and cut the halves into quarters, leaving the green still attached to the white – when the onions are dropped into chilled water the green leaves will fan out like a flower. Cut the cucumber into fine 5 cm / 2 inch batons.

6 Once the duck is dry it is ready for roasting. Preheat the oven to 200°C/400°F/gas mark 6. Place the duck on a rack in a roasting tray, or better still on a rotisserie in your oven. Put about 600 ml / 1 pint of water in the roasting tray – this will help to steam the duck as it roasts.

7 Roast the duck, breast side down, for the first 30 minutes, then carefully turn the duck onto its back and roast for 15 minutes. Finally, turn it breast side down again and roast for 15 minutes.

8 Using a skewer, prick the leg of the duck. If the liquid runs out clear, it is cooked. Increase the heat to 220°C/425°F/gas mark 7 and cook for 10–15 minutes to crisp up the skin.

9 Remove the duck from the oven and transfer to a suitable serving dish, then leave to rest for 10 minutes or so in a warm place or on top of the stove.

10 To serve the duck, it is the job of the host or hostess to keep thinly slicing the duck to order. Spread each pancake with some of the hoisin sauce, add some spring onion and cucumber to taste, top with a couple of very thin slices of the duck, then roll the pancake up and eat.

Mandarin pancakes

450 g / 1 lb plain flour, plus extra for dusting
300 ml / 10 fl oz boiling water
1 small sherry glass of vegetable oil

1 Sift the flour into a bowl.

2 Mix the boiling water with the oil and slowly pour into the flour, stirring all the while until you have a dough. Then dive in with your hands and knead the dough until it is smooth and firm.

3 Divide the dough into equal golf ball-sized portions. Dust with a little flour and roll into very thin disks about 15 cm / 6 inches in diameter, then brush lightly with oil.

4 Heat a heavy-based frying pan and cook each pancake until air bubbles appear on the surface, then turn it over and repeat on the other side. Remove from the pan and repeat until all the pancakes are cooked. Layer the pancakes between greaseproof paper and store in a cool place until required.

5 When ready to serve, briefly reheat the pancakes in a bamboo steamer over a pan of simmering water.

Tea-smoked duck

1 plump free-range duck, about 2.5 kg/
    5½ lb in weight, giblets, neck and feet
    removed and discarded
2 teacups uncooked long grain rice
1 teacup Chinese green tea leaves
peel of 1 orange, dried in a low oven
2 tablespoons soft brown sugar
sea salt and freshly ground black pepper
vegetable oil, for deep-frying
dips and sauces, to serve

1 Heat a large pan of boiling water and plunge
the duck in for 2 minutes, turning the duck so
that all sides are blanched. Remove the duck,
discard the water and pat the duck dry. Rub salt
and pepper liberally all over the duck and inside
the cavity, then wrap the duck in clingfilm and
refrigerate for 5 or 6 hours.

2 Meanwhile, prepare your smoking pack. Take
3 large equal-sized pieces of tin foil and lay them
on top of one another to create 3 layers. Sprinkle

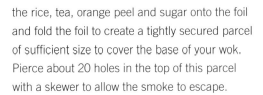

the rice, tea, orange peel and sugar onto the foil
and fold the foil to create a tightly secured parcel
of sufficient size to cover the base of your wok.
Pierce about 20 holes in the top of this parcel
with a skewer to allow the smoke to escape.

3 Place the parcel in the bottom of the wok and
place a trivet or cake cooling rack over it, but
inside the wok to allow for a secure lid. Heat the
wok until the parcel begins to smoke, then
reduce the heat.

4 Place the duck, breast side down, on the rack
or trivet, cover tightly with a well-fitting lid or foil
so that the smoke cannot escape and smoke for
10–15 minutes, then turn the duck onto its back
and continue smoking for another 10–15 minutes.

5 Next, transfer the duck to a large bamboo
steamer and cover with the lid or foil. Place over
a pan of gently boiling water and steam for about
1½ hours, topping up the pan with boiling water
when necessary.

6 To test if the duck is cooked, pierce one of the
legs with a skewer: if a clear liquid runs out the
duck is cooked; if not, continue steaming until it
is cooked. Remove the duck from the steamer
and pat dry with plenty of kitchen paper.

7 Heat sufficient oil for deep-frying in a large
pan, then fry the duck until it is crispy and
golden, turning the duck from time to time.
Carefully remove from the pan and drain on
kitchen paper.

8 Serving notes: The Chinese, using a cleaver,
would cut the whole duck, bones and all, into
bite-sized pieces and dip them into soy sauce,
chilli sauce, hoisin sauce or similar.

Left *Good-looking ducks for sale at Chaoyang wholesale
market.* Opposite *An elderly farmer with his pipe and
cigarette in Yongning.*

Above *No plastic-wrapped chicken here – you get the whole chicken and nothing but the chicken.*

Lemon chicken

4 skinless, boneless chicken breasts

flour, to coat the chicken

4 egg yolks

2 heaped teaspoons cornflour mixed with a little cold water to the consistency of single cream

sea salt and freshly ground black pepper

vegetable oil, for deep-frying

6 spring onions, trimmed and chopped, to garnish

for the sauce

juice of 3 or 4 lemons

225 ml / 8 fl oz chicken stock

2 tablespoons honey

1 tablespoon brown sugar

1 cm / ½ inch piece fresh root ginger, peeled and grated

2 heaped teaspoons cornflour mixed with a little cold water to the consistency of single cream

1 To make the sauce, mix the lemon juice with the stock, honey, sugar and ginger. Stir in the cornflour mixture and cook over a low heat, stirring from time to time, until the sauce thickens, then put to one side.

2 Lightly flour the chicken breasts and flatten them out a little with a rolling pin.

3 To make a coating batter, beat the egg yolks into the cornflour mixture and season with salt and pepper.

4 Heat sufficient oil for deep-frying in a pan, then fry the chicken gently until golden. Drain on kitchen paper and put to one side in a warm place.

5 Reheat the sauce. Slice each chicken breast into 3 or 4 pieces and place on a serving dish. Pour the sauce over the chicken, garnish with chopped spring onions and serve.

Baked chicken wings

1.5 kg / 3½ lb chicken wings

for the marinade
1 garlic clove, peeled and very finely
  chopped
2.5 cm / 1 inch piece fresh root ginger,
  peeled and grated
2 teaspoons brown sugar
a good dash of rice wine, sake or dry
  sherry
2 or 3 tablespoons vegetable oil
1 overflowing tablespoon honey
sea salt and freshly ground black pepper

1 Mix all the ingredients for the marinade in a bowl.

2 Cut off and discard the wing tips from the chicken wings. Using a very sharp knife, cut the meat free from the bone, pushing it down to the thick end, then turn the meat inside out around the top of the bone so that it resembles a little drumstick. Place in the marinade and turn to coat, then leave in the fridge overnight.

3 When ready to cook, preheat the oven to 180°C / 350°F / gas mark 4. Put the chicken wings and the marinade into a baking tray and bake for 35–40 minutes, or until cooked, basting from time to time. This makes excellent and unusual finger food.

Garlic chicken

1 egg white, beaten
1 heaped teaspoon cornflour
2 or 3 tablespoons rice wine, sake or dry
  sherry
4 small skinless, boneless chicken
  breasts, about 500 g / 1 lb 2 oz in
  weight, cut into thin strips
sesame oil
vegetable oil, for stir-frying

for the sauce
3.5 cm / 1½ inch piece fresh root ginger,
  peeled and grated
6 fat garlic cloves, peeled and finely
  crushed
1 teaspoon chilli paste
1 tablespoon soft brown sugar
1 teaspoon cornflour mixed with a little
  cold water to the consistency of single
  cream
a dash of white rice vinegar
2 or 3 tablespoons rice wine, sake or dry
  sherry
2 or 3 tablespoons light soy sauce

1 Make a batter from the egg white, cornflour and rice wine, sake or sherry.

2 Add the chicken strips to the batter, stir well so that they are well coated and leave for 30–40 minutes at room temperature.

3 Heat a wok, add a little vegetable oil and gently stir-fry the ginger and garlic for about 30 seconds.

4 Add the chicken and stir-fry until cooked and golden. Remove from the wok and keep warm in a serving dish.

5 Mix all the remaining sauce ingredients with a dash of vegetable oil, add to the wok and stir until the sauce is hot and slightly thickened. Stir in a few dashes of sesame oil, pour over the chicken and serve.

Chicken in hot sauce, Sichuan style

4 skinless, boneless chicken breasts, cut
 into 2.5 cm / 1 inch cubes
2.5 cm / 1 inch piece fresh root ginger,
 peeled and finely chopped
4 spring onions, trimmed and sliced
 diagonally into 1 cm / ½ inch lengths
3 garlic cloves, peeled and finely chopped
1 bag of baby spinach leaves, washed
 and dried
vegetable oil, for stir-frying

for the marinade

1 tablespoon light soy sauce
1 dessertspoon rice wine, sake or dry
 sherry
2 tablespoons water
2 teaspoons cornflour
5 tablespoons vegetable oil

for the sauce

1 dessertspoon rice wine, sake or dry
 sherry
1 dessertspoon light soy sauce
a few drops of sesame oil
1 dessertspoon red wine vinegar or red
 Chinese vinegar
3 teaspoons sugar
2 tablespoons water
2 teaspoons cornflour
1 tablespoon chilli sauce
1 teaspoon freshly ground Sichuan
 pepper

1 Mix all the ingredients for the marinade in a bowl, add the chicken and turn to coat, then leave for 30 minutes.

2 Mix all the ingredients for the sauce in a bowl and put to one side.

3 Heat a wok, add a little vegetable oil and stir-fry the chicken, stirring continuously to prevent the chicken from sticking.

4 When the chicken is cooked, stir in the ginger, spring onions and garlic. Add the sauce mixture and keep stir-frying until you have a thick sauce. Remove from the heat and put to one side in a warm place.

5 Heat a little oil in another pan and swiftly stir-fry the spinach until it has wilted. Pile the spinach in a serving dish, pour the chicken and sauce over the top and serve.

Below *An incense burner in the Temple Kitchen restaurant, housed in the White Pagoda Temple, Beihai Park, Beijing.* **Opposite** *The kitchen of this Sichuan restaurant was jolly hot and very busy.*

Above *The fearless beekeeper at work in the countryside outside Beijing.*

Deep-fried chicken, on the bone, with honey and chilli sauce

1 chicken, about 1.5 kg / 3½ lb in weight
plain flour, to coat the chicken
1 red onion, peeled and very finely diced
2.5 cm / 1 inch piece fresh root ginger,
    peeled and finely chopped
sea salt
vegetable oil, for frying

for the sauce
2 teaspoons cornflour mixed with a little
    cold water to the consistency of single
    cream
2 full tablespoons honey
1 tablespoon chilli sauce
juice of 2 lemons
2 tablespoons dark soy sauce

1 Chop the chicken into bite-sized pieces and dredge in lightly salted flour. (If you find it too fiddly dealing with the bones you can make this dish with chunks of chicken breast, but the taste will be nowhere near as good! Remember that the Chinese, along with most Asian people, cannot afford the luxury of using just the chicken breasts and discarding the rest.)

2 Mix all the ingredients for the sauce in a bowl.

3 Heat a wok, add a little oil and sauté the onion and ginger until they are soft.

4 Whisking all the while, add the sauce mixture and cook until it boils and thickens. Transfer the sauce to a bowl and keep it warm.

5 Wipe out the wok, then heat enough oil for deep-frying and fry the chicken pieces in two or three batches until they are tender and golden (about 5–6 minutes).

6 Drain the chicken on kitchen paper, then transfer to a hot serving plate or dish, pour the sauce over the chicken and serve.

Chicken with mango and ginger

4 skinless, boneless chicken breasts, cut into thin strips
5 cm / 2 inch piece fresh root ginger, peeled and cut into fine strips
200 ml / 7 fl oz water
3 tablespoons white wine vinegar
3 tablespoons rice wine, sake or dry sherry
1 tablespoon dark soy sauce
2 teaspoons sugar
2 teaspoons cornflour
½ chicken stock cube, crumbled
1 teaspoon sesame oil
8 or 10 spring onions, trimmed and sliced diagonally into 1 cm / ½ inch lengths (use the white and the green)
1 ripe mango, peeled and sliced
vegetable oil, for frying

for the batter

1 heaped tablespoon plain flour
200 ml / 7 fl oz water
a good pinch of baking powder
a good pinch of sea salt

1 Whisk together all the ingredients for the batter and leave to stand for about 15 minutes. If the mixture is a bit thick, add a little more water.

2 Coat the chicken strips in the batter mixture and put to one side while you heat some vegetable oil in a wok. Add the chicken pieces a few at a time and cook until golden brown (about 4–5 minutes). Drain the chicken on kitchen paper.

3 Wipe out the wok, add a little more oil and bring to a medium heat. Add the ginger and stir-fry until it browns slightly.

4 Mix the remaining water, the vinegar, rice wine, sake or sherry, the soy sauce, sugar, cornflour, stock cube and sesame oil in a bowl. Add to the ginger and heat, stirring continuously, until the mixture boils.

5 Add the spring onions and simmer the mixture for a couple of minutes, then add the chicken and mango to the pan with the sauce and stir until all the ingredients are thoroughly mixed and hot. Transfer to a serving dish and serve.

Left *A vendor selling ginger waits for customers in a street market in Beijing.*

Deep-fried crispy poussin with cucumber and pineapple salad

As with all cooking, preparation and planning is everything – 40 minutes preparation in the calm of the morning will leave you with a 10-minute task at dinner time.

4 small poussins
plain flour, for coating the poussins
sea salt
peanut oil, for deep-frying

for the marinade
1 tablespoon white rice vinegar
2 tablespoons honey
2 tablespoons soy sauce
2 tablespoons rice wine, sake or dry
    sherry
2 tablespoons dark treacle or molasses

for the cucumber and pineapple salad
1 cucumber, peeled, halved lengthways
    and deseeded
1 small ripe pineapple, peeled and cut
    into 1 cm / ½ inch cubes
2 tablespoons fish sauce
a pinch of ground chilli or dried chilli
    flakes

1 First make the salad. Cut the cucumber into little half moon slices and mix with the pineapple cubes. Add the fish sauce and ground chilli or chilli flakes, then cover and refrigerate until needed.

2 Meanwhile, back at the early morning coalface, pop the poussins into a suitably large saucepan. Pour over boiling water to just cover the birds, cover with a lid and simmer for about 30 minutes.

3 Drain the poussins carefully, dry thoroughly with kitchen paper and put to one side to cool.

4 Meanwhile, mix all the ingredients for the marinade in a bowl.

5 Put a rack in a roasting tray, place the poussins on the rack and paint the marinade all over them, then leave to dry. Once the poussins are dry, repeat the process until the marinade is used up. Now you can forget about it until the evening.

6 When ready to cook, season some flour with salt and rub well into the skin of the poussins.

7 Heat enough oil for deep-frying and fry the poussins individually until crispy and golden, then drain on kitchen paper. Serve with the cucumber and pineapple salad.

Opposite Fresh pineapple is often sold by the roadside, and it's deliciously juicy.

Fish
and
Shellfish

Above left to right *Great, juicy prawns; stir-fried prawns with peppers (page 78); these huge mussels were on sale at the Chaoyang wholesale market.*

Fish and Shellfish

Steaming, grilling or stir-frying are the most popular methods of cooking fish and shellfish in China and, to retain their fresh juiciness, they are cooked only briefly, often after having been marinated.

As with poultry, the Chinese waste nothing of the fish, eating the head, eyes, lips and even the fins.

Freshwater fish is a great favourite, and when it comes to other sea creatures, nothing is safe – sea slugs, sea snails and

Above *A fish vendor waits for customers in the Chaoyang wholesale market.*

turtles are just some of the delicacies they enjoy from the deep.

A word about prawns: always buy and use fresh prawns or frozen fresh prawns. Don't buy ready-cooked prawns.

To prepare large, raw prawns, once they are shelled run a sharp knife down the centre of the back of each prawn and remove the dark intestinal cord. The cut will also make the prawns open out, or 'butterfly', when they are cooked. Rinse the prawns well before use.

Deep-fried shell-on prawns

450 g / 1 lb large raw tiger prawns in the
    shell, with heads
sea salt, to taste
chilli sauce
vegetable oil, for deep-frying

for the marinade

2 x 2.5 cm / 1 inch pieces fresh root
    ginger, peeled and very finely chopped
a good dash of rice wine, sake or dry
    sherry
1 heaped teaspoon cornflour

for the garnish

coarsely chopped coriander leaves
lemon or lime wedges

1 Put all the ingredients for the marinade in a bowl and mix to a smooth paste.

2 Add the prawns and turn to coat them on both sides, then marinate in the fridge for 1 hour.

3 Heat sufficient oil for deep-frying in a wok or deep-fat fryer (to see if it is at the right temperature drop in a cube of bread – if it sizzles, the oil is hot enough). Add the prawns and fry for about 1 minute, or until they have turned beautifully pink. Remove the prawns from the oil and drain on kitchen paper. Strain the oil into another pan for future use and wipe out the wok.

4 Return the prawns to the wok, season with salt and add enough chilli sauce to coat the prawns, then stir-fry for a further minute, mixing well.

5 Transfer to a serving dish, garnish with coriander leaves and serve immediately with the lemon or lime wedges.

Below *Large raw tiger prawns.*

Above *A cook at work in a Sichuan restaurant.*

Stir-fried prawns with green peas

450 g / 1 lb large raw tiger prawns, head
    and shell removed but tail left on, and
    deveined
350 g / 12 oz small frozen peas, defrosted
4 spring onions, trimmed and finely
    chopped
2.5 cm / 1 inch piece fresh root ginger,
    peeled and finely chopped
sea salt, to taste
a dash of rice wine, sake or dry sherry
vegetable oil, for stir-frying

for the marinade
2 egg whites
4 teaspoons cornflour

1 Mix the ingredients for the marinade in a bowl, toss the prawns in it and marinate in the fridge for 1 hour.

2 Heat a wok, add a little oil and stir-fry the prawns for about 1 minute. Remove the prawns, drain on kitchen paper and put to one side.

3 Add the peas, spring onions, ginger and salt to the wok and stir-fry for about 2 minutes.

4 Return the prawns to the wok, add a dash of rice wine, sake or sherry and stir-fry for about 2 minutes, then serve immediately.

Whole bream, plump grey mullet or carp in sweet and sour sauce

1 fish, about 1 kg/2¼ lb, scaled, gutted and all fins, including tail if wished, removed (the head can also be removed if preferred, although personally I like to leave the head and tail on, it is more authentic and looks better on the plate!)

sea salt

a little plain flour, to coat the fish

vegetable oil, for shallow-frying

for the stir-fried vegetables

2 or 3 spring onions, trimmed and finely chopped

2 thin slices peeled fresh root ginger, finely chopped

1 garlic clove, peeled and finely chopped

½ small can bamboo shoots, thinly sliced, rinsed and dried

50 g/2 oz water chestnuts, thinly sliced, rinsed and dried

1 red pepper, deseeded and pith removed, cut into very thin strips, about 3.5 cm/1½ inches long

1 small sherry glass of white wine vinegar

for the sauce

a good dash of rice wine, sake or dry sherry

150 ml/5 fl oz fish stock

2 dessertspoons caster sugar

a couple of shakes of soy sauce

2 teaspoons cornflour

at least 1 teaspoon chilli sauce (more if you like it spicy)

1 Make several diagonal cuts on each side of the fish and rub in salt, then dredge the fish in flour to coat it and shake off any excess.

2 Heat a wok or large frying pan, add some oil and gently fry the fish for 3–4 minutes on each side until browned and crispy. Transfer the fish to a suitable serving platter and keep warm.

3 Wipe the wok clean with a piece of kitchen paper and heat some fresh oil. Stir-fry all the vegetables for about 2 minutes, then season with salt to taste and the vinegar.

4 Mix all the ingredients for the sauce in a bowl until smooth. Add the sauce to the vegetables and continue cooking, stirring all the time, until the sauce thickens. Pour over the fish and serve immediately.

Opposite *I cooked these fish in the kitchen of the Hakka restaurant, which serves food of the Han people.*

Above *The quantity, variety and quality of fish for sale in the markets is amazing.*

Fried fish with ginger sauce

750 g / 1 lb 10 oz whole red mullet, red
   snapper or sea bass, scaled, gutted
   and fins removed, but head and tail
   left on
125 g / 4½ oz plain flour, plus extra to
   coat the fish
a good pinch of sea salt
vegetable oil, for deep-frying
1 quantity Ginger sauce (see page 181)

1 Slash the fish several times on both sides in a criss-cross pattern.

2 Mix the flour, salt and a dash of vegetable oil with enough cold water to make a smooth batter.

3 Dredge the fish in some flour, shake off the excess and coat the fish with the batter.

4 Heat sufficient oil for deep-frying in a wok or pan, and fry the fish until it is golden brown all over and the skin is crispy.

5 Meanwhile, heat the ginger sauce. Drain the fish on kitchen paper and serve with the hot ginger sauce.

Stir-fried chilli crab or lobster in the shell

This is a messy but delicious way to eat a fresh crab. You will need shellfish picks, fingerbowls and lots of paper napkins. You will also need a seriously good fishmonger who can provide you with a really fleshy, large crab or lobster and who will be prepared to despatch it for you, remove the inedible bits and then chop the main body and the large claws into large pieces. It is worth the effort, I assure you!

1 large crab or lobster, about 2 kg/4½ lb,
    or 2 smaller ones of at least 1 kg/
    2¼ lb each
6 hot red chillies, deseeded and finely
    sliced lengthways
2 garlic cloves, peeled and finely chopped
2 thin slices peeled fresh root ginger,
    finely chopped
1½ teaspoons cornflour
125 ml/4 fl oz water
5 or 6 spring onions, trimmed and
    chopped
1 teaspoon mild chilli powder
1 heaped teaspoon soft brown sugar
peanut oil, for stir-frying

1 Heat a large wok, add a little oil and stir-fry the crab or lobster for 6–8 minutes.

2 Strain off any excess oil, add the sliced chillies, the garlic and ginger and stir-fry for about 30 seconds.

3 Mix the cornflour with the water, then add to the wok with the spring onions, chilli powder and sugar and cook, stirring all the time, until the sauce thickens, then serve.

Below *Tank upon tank of shellfish, crustacea and other delights of the deep at this lively fish market.*

Stir-fried prawns with peppers

250 g / 9 oz large raw tiger prawns, head
and shell removed but tail left on, and
deveined

2.5 cm / 1 inch piece fresh root ginger,
peeled and finely chopped

1 red pepper and 1 green pepper,
deseeded and pith removed, sliced
into strips

3 spring onions, trimmed and sliced
diagonally into 2.5 cm / 1 inch lengths

100 g / 3½ oz water chestnuts, thinly
sliced, rinsed and dried

1 tablespoon rice wine, sake or dry sherry

1 tablespoon dark soy sauce

1 teaspoon cornflour mixed with a little
cold water to a smooth paste

a good pinch of dried chilli flakes

vegetable oil, for frying

1 Heat a wok, add a little oil and stir-fry the prawns for
2–3 minutes, then remove from the wok and drain on
kitchen paper.

2 Add the ginger, pepper strips and spring onions to the
wok and stir-fry for 3 minutes or so, then add the water
chestnuts.

3 Mix the rice wine, sake or sherry and the soy sauce in
a small bowl and stir in the cornflour mixture. Add to the
wok and stir until well mixed.

4 Return the prawns to the wok, add the chilli flakes and
cook, stirring, until the sauce has thickened.

5 Transfer to a warm serving dish and serve.

Grilled monkfish with ginger and soy sauce

4 monkfish fillets, skinned right down to
the flesh – monkfish has a membrane
that must be removed or the fillets
could become tough

for the marinade
2 x 2.5 cm / 1 inch pieces fresh root
ginger, peeled and grated
1 fat garlic clove, peeled and finely
chopped
120 ml / 4 fl oz light soy sauce
white pepper, to taste

1 Mix all the ingredients for the marinade in a bowl. Add the monkfish fillets and marinate in the fridge for about 4 hours, turning them from time to time.

2 Preheat the grill to hot and line the grill pan with foil to catch any juices.

3 Place the monkfish fillets under the grill and grill for about 5 minutes on each side, basting with the marinade throughout the grilling process.

4 Serve the monkfish with the juices from the grill pan poured over them.

Steamed scallops or monkfish with black bean sauce

This can also work wonderfully with sea bass fillets or fresh lobster cut in half lengthways.

500–750 g / 1 lb 2 oz–1 lb 10 oz fresh
shelled scallops or monkfish
a dash of vegetable oil
a sherry glass of rice wine, sake or dry
sherry
½ teaspoon caster sugar
a couple of dashes of light soy sauce
2 thin slices peeled fresh root ginger, cut
into very thin strips
2 or 3 spring onions, trimmed and cut
into 5 cm / 2 inch batons, then cut into
4 lengthways
2 tablespoons black bean sauce
fresh coriander leaves, to garnish

1 Place the scallops or monkfish on a lightly oiled plate or dish. Cover the fish with all the remaining ingredients except the coriander and pop into your electric steamer for 5–10 minutes.

2 Alternatively, fill your wok with water, buy a nice large bamboo steamer, place the plate of fish and vegetables in the steamer, cover with a lid and cook for about 10 minutes.

3 Garnish with the coriander and serve.

Above *Fresh, juicy scallops.*

Spicy scallops

4 spring onions, trimmed and sliced
 diagonally into 2.5 cm / 1 inch lengths
500 g / 1 lb 2 oz fresh shelled scallops
peanut oil, for stir-frying

for the sauce
250 ml / 8½ fl oz fish stock
sea salt
several dashes of hot red pepper sauce,
 to taste
½ teaspoon ground ginger
50 g / 2 oz water chestnuts, thinly sliced,
 rinsed and dried
1 tablespoon cornflour mixed with 50 ml /
 2 fl oz rice wine or dry white wine

1 Heat a wok or shallow pan, add a little oil and stir-fry
the spring onions until they are soft.

2 Add the scallops and stir-fry for a further minute.

3 Add all the sauce ingredients and stir-fry until the
sauce thickens, then serve.

Above *Chaoyang wholesale market* **Opposite** *These beautiful fish couldn't have been fresher and I bet they tasted great.*

Pan-fried whole fish with sesame oil and spring onions

1 whole fish – red snapper, red mullet or
   bream, scaled, gutted and fins
   removed, but head and tail left on
a dash of rice wine, sake or dry sherry
a little plain flour, to coat the fish
3 tablespoons sesame oil
8 or 10 spring onions, trimmed and
   sliced diagonally into 2.5 cm / 1 inch
   lengths
sea salt and freshly ground black pepper
vegetable oil, for frying

1 Make several diagonal cuts on each side of the fish, right down to the bone. Rub in the rice wine, sake or dry sherry and salt and pepper, then roll the fish in the flour to coat it and shake off any excess.

2 Heat a large frying pan, add a little vegetable oil and fry the fish for 7–8 minutes on each side until the skin is crispy and golden brown. Transfer the fish to a warm serving platter and keep warm.

3 Heat the sesame oil in a small pan and stir-fry the spring onions until they have softened.

4 Pour the oil and onions over the fish and serve.

Seared scallops with spinach

300 g / 11 oz fresh shelled scallops,
    sliced in half
1 teaspoon five-spice powder (see page
    178)
150 g / 5 oz baby spinach leaves, washed
    and dried
sea salt
vegetable oil, for frying

for the sauce
2 fat garlic cloves, peeled and finely
    chopped
5 cm / 2 inch piece fresh root ginger,
    peeled and finely chopped
2 or 3 tablespoons rice wine, sake or dry
    sherry
2 tablespoons light soy sauce
2 teaspoons sesame oil

1 Season the scallops with the five-spice powder and a little salt.

2 Heat a large frying pan and pour in a little vegetable oil. Sear the scallops for a minute or so on each side until they take on some colour, then remove from the pan and keep warm.

3 Mix all the ingredients for the sauce in a bowl. Add the sauce to the pan and cook, stirring continuously, for 3–4 minutes.

4 Return the scallops to the pan, add the spinach and stir-fry for 1–2 minutes until the spinach has wilted, then serve at once.

Squid in black bean sauce

350 g / 12 oz squid tubes, cleaned
1 green pepper and 1 red pepper, each
    deseeded and pith removed, cut into
    2.5 cm / 1 inch squares
1 garlic clove, peeled and finely chopped
4 or 5 spring onions, trimmed and finely
    chopped
1 cm / ½ inch piece fresh root ginger,
    peeled and finely chopped
1 tablespoon rice wine, sake or dry sherry
1 tablespoon black bean sauce
sea salt, to taste
vegetable oil, for stir-frying
a few drops of sesame oil, to finish

1 Cut open each squid tube lengthways to form a flat sheet and score the inside of the squid in a criss-cross pattern, then cut into 3.5 cm / 1⅙ inch squares.

2 Fill a pan with lightly salted water and bring to the boil. Drop in the squid and blanch for about 1 minute. Remove the squid, drain and dry on kitchen paper.

3 Next, heat a wok, add a little vegetable oil and stir-fry the peppers for a minute or two.

4 Add the garlic, spring onions, ginger, salt and squid and continue to stir-fry for another 2 minutes.

5 Add the rice wine, sake or dry sherry and the black bean sauce and stir until warmed through.

6 Transfer the whole lot to a warm serving dish, add a few drops of sesame oil and serve hot.

Fried squid with bok choi

1.5 kg / 3½ lb squid tubes, cleaned

1 red onion, peeled and very finely sliced

2 stringed celery sticks, about 15 cm /
6 inches long, chopped into 2.5 cm /
1 inch batons cut on the diagonal

1.5 kg / 3½ lb bok choi, green leaves
ripped coarsely into large pieces and
white stem cut into thin slices

6 spring onions, trimmed and sliced
diagonally into 2.5 cm / 1 inch lengths

2.5 cm / 1 inch piece fresh root ginger,
peeled and grated

vegetable oil, for frying

for the sauce

1 tablespoon cornflour

150 ml / 5 fl oz water

2 tablespoons rice wine, sake or dry
sherry

2 fish stock cubes, crumbled

4 tablespoons oyster sauce

2 tablespoons light soy sauce

a couple of dashes of sesame oil

1 teaspoon caster sugar

½ teaspoon sea salt

1 Cut open each squid tube lengthways to form a flat sheet and score the inside of the squid in a criss-cross pattern. Not only does this tenderise the squid, but it makes it curl attractively when cooked.

2 Heat a wok, add a little vegetable oil and stir-fry the squid until it curls. Remove the squid, drain on kitchen paper and put to one side.

3 Add a little more oil to the wok and add the red onion, celery, bok choi, spring onions and ginger and stir-fry for 3–4 minutes.

4 Meanwhile, mix all the ingredients for the sauce in a bowl. Stir the sauce into the vegetables and cook, stirring all the time, until the sauce boils and thickens.

5 Return the squid to the wok to heat through, then serve.

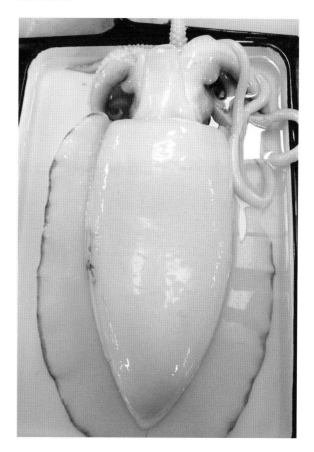

Right What a magnificent specimen!

Steamed prawns with soy chilli dip

For the weight-conscious, this is an absolute breeze and jolly delicious. The soy chilli dip is great with any steamed fish.

1 kg/2¼ lb large raw tiger prawns in the
    shell

for the soy chilli dip
1 green chilli and 1 red chilli, each
    deseeded and finely chopped
1 tablespoon vegetable oil
light soy sauce

1 To make the dip, put the chillies in a small bowl with the vegetable oil and add enough soy sauce to cover the ingredients and then a little dash more. Leave in the fridge for 30 minutes before using.

2 Steam the prawns in an electric or bamboo steamer over rapidly boiling water for 5–7 minutes and serve with the dipping sauce.

Stir-fried mixed seafood

300 g/11 oz squid tubes, cleaned
130 g can water chestnuts, rinsed and
    dried
130 g can bamboo shoots, rinsed and
    dried
8 shallots, peeled and thinly sliced
    diagonally
2 stringed celery sticks, cut diagonally
    into 2.5 cm/1 inch lengths
300 g/11 oz fresh shelled scallops
300 g/11 oz large raw tiger prawns, head
    and shell removed but tail left on, and
    deveined
vegetable oil, for stir-frying

for the sauce
1 teaspoon cornflour mixed with a little
    cold water to a smooth paste
1 chicken stock cube, dissolved in
    150 ml/5 fl oz hot water
2 tablespoons rice wine, sake or dry
    sherry
1 teaspoon sesame oil
2 tablespoons light soy sauce

1 Cut open each squid tube lengthways to form a flat sheet and score the inside of the squid in a criss-cross pattern, then cut into 2.5 cm/1 inch squares.

2 Cut the water chestnuts in half and thinly slice the bamboo shoots.

3 Heat a wok, add a little vegetable oil and stir-fry all the vegetables for a couple of minutes or so, then remove from the wok, drain on kitchen paper and keep warm.

4 Add a little more oil to the wok and stir-fry the scallops, squid and prawns for a couple of minutes.

5 Stir all the sauce ingredients into the wok and stir-fry until the sauce is boiling and has thickened.

6 Return the vegetables to the wok and cook for a further minute, then serve hot.

Beef

Above left to right *A hotpot or steamboat; cooking the beef (page 94); cooking the vegetables and bean curd.*

Beef

Sichuan cuisine has a good range of beef dishes, and they are popular too among the Chinese Muslims, but elsewhere pork is far more commonly found. But, in fact, most pork dishes can be made with beef instead. However, unlike pork, beef is hardly ever diced, but is cut into thin slices or strips.

As with all luxury items like pork, beef, chicken, duck, shellfish, in the Chinese kitchen a little goes a long way. Whereas we in the West need half a cow to roast on Sundays, with two tons of roasted potatoes and a sack of Brussels sprouts, the Chinese, who are not parsimonious, but good husbanders of resources, will use these ingredients to brighten up and flavour fundamental dishes of noodles or rice.

The Mongolian beef hotpot on page 94 is a truly memorable dish and just the thing to entertain a crowd of mates with. In China the beef will have been severely chilled and sliced very thinly to make a little go a long way and it also cooks quickly.

Below *These lotus roots were jolly good in my hotpot at the Little Winter hotpot restaurant in Ghost Street.*

Above *A farmer with his horse in the countryside outside Beijing.*

Twice-cooked simmered beef

750 g / 1 lb 10 oz piece stewing beef, most of the fat trimmed off, but not all
1 thick slices peeled fresh root ginger
1 sherry glass of rice wine, sake or dry sherry
50 ml / 2 fl oz dark soy sauce
1 heaped tablespoon soft brown sugar
vegetable oil, for frying
sesame oil, to finish

1 Put the beef, ginger and rice wine, sake or sherry into a large pan, add just enough water to cover the beef and bring to the boil. Reduce the heat to a simmer, skim off any fat that has floated to the surface, cover the pan and simmer gently for 40–45 minutes.

2 Remove the beef from the pan and leave to go cold. Reserve the cooking liquid. When the beef is cold, cut it into thin slices. Reheat the broth.

3 Heat a wok or frying pan, add a little vegetable oil and stir-fry the beef for about 1 minute, then add the soy sauce, sugar and the reserved broth. Cover the wok or pan and simmer for 10 minutes, or until the beef is tender and warmed through.

4 Pour into a serving dish and sprinkle (I refuse to use the word drizzle!) a few drops of sesame oil to float on top of the dish.

Above *This shop in Yongning sold a bit of everything, including some interesting cooking utensils.*

Chinese simmered beef with carrots

2 garlic cloves, peeled and crushed

2 thin slices peeled fresh root ginger, finely chopped

2 spring onions, trimmed and coarsely chopped

750 g / 1 lb 10 oz stewing beef, fat trimmed off, and cut into 1 cm / ½ inch squares

40 ml / 1½ fl oz dark soy sauce

1 tablespoon soft brown sugar

a dash of rice wine, sake or dry sherry

½ teaspoon five-spice powder (see page 178)

450 g / 1 lb young carrots, peeled

vegetable oil, for frying

1 Heat some oil in a heavy pan or casserole and stir-fry the garlic, ginger and spring onions until golden brown.

2 Add the beef and all the remaining ingredients except the carrots, then pour in enough cold water to cover the meat.

3 Bring to the boil and skim off any foam, then reduce the heat and simmer gently, partially covered, for about 1½ hours.

4 Meanwhile, cut the carrots lengthways into slices, then cut the slices diagonally into diamond shapes.

5 After the beef has been simmering for about 1 hour, add the carrots and continue to cook for a further 30 minutes until the meat and the carrots are tender.

Mongolian beef hotpot

This is a spectacular dish that ranks alongside the famous Peking Duck (see page 54). All the guests cook their own food by using what is known as a hotpot or a steamboat – normally quite an ornate sort of a fondue dish that has a metholated spirit-fired burner in the middle (you could, of course, use a regular fondue set). Although this recipe is for beef, you could substitute lamb or fillet of pork.

You will also need to buy some little wire baskets (available from Chinese stores) for lowering ingredients into the broth, as you will see from the method below.

1.5 kg / 3½ lb fillet steak, membrane
    trimmed off
450 g / 1 lb baby spinach leaves,
    washed and dried
1 kg / 2¼ lb Chinese cabbage, either
    the pale green Chinese leaves, or,
    for preference, dark green-leaved
    bok choi (or a mixture of both), cut
    into pieces, stalk and all
2 or 3 blocks of firm bean curd, cut
    into cubes
100 g / 3½ oz transparent rice noodles
2.5 litres / 4 pints clear beef stock (you
    can use stock cubes)

to serve
You will also need several little bowls
    of sauces such as chilli sauce,
    hoisin sauce, dark soy sauce and
    light soy sauce, with some
    garnishes of finely chopped spring
    onions, ginger and garlic

1 Place the fillet of beef into the freezer for 1 hour as this will make the beef easier to slice. Then, using a very sharp knife, cut the beef into wafer-thin slices and arrange them on a large serving dish. Make sure all the slices are separate from each other for ease of picking up.

2 Place the steamboat in the middle of the table and surround with the vegetables, beef, bean curd, dipping sauces and garnishes.

3 Add the beef stock to the steamboat and bring to a boil, then reduce the heat to a slow, rolling simmer. (Alternatively, if using a fondue set, heat the stock in a pan first.)

4 Using chopsticks, each guest picks up a couple of slices of beef, pops them into the broth for a few seconds, then lifts them out with the little baskets and dips them into the sauce of their choice. A nice thing to do is to cook a couple of slices of beef and then a little basket full of vegetables and bean curd (see page 90).

5 When all the beef has been eaten, add the remaining vegetables with the noodles into what will by now be a very rich broth, cook for a few minutes and serve as a soup to finish the meal.

Skewered beef with sweet chilli sauce dip

500 g / 1 lb 2 oz sirloin steak, fat trimmed
   off

for the marinade

100 ml / 3½ fl oz dark soy sauce

2 garlic cloves, peeled and very finely
   chopped

2.5 cm / 1 inch piece fresh root ginger,
   peeled and very finely chopped

2 teaspoons cornflour mixed with a little
   cold water to the consistency of single
   cream

150 ml / 5 fl oz rice wine, sake or dry
   sherry

for the dipping sauce

150 ml / 5 fl oz sweet chilli sauce

a couple of dashes of dark soy sauce

½ teaspoon sesame oil

1 Mix all the ingredients for the marinade in a large
shallow dish.

2 Cut the beef into thin strips about 8 mm / ⅓ inch wide
and 15 cm / 6 inches long. Thread the strips onto
skewers, place in the marinade and turn to coat the
meat, then leave in the fridge for 1 hour.

3 Place the skewers under a hot grill and cook for about
2 minutes on each side, making sure the beef is slightly
pink inside.

4 Meanwhile, mix all the ingredients for the dipping
sauce and serve with the beef.

Below *A vendor in Wangfujing night market sells grasshoppers, silk
worm cocoons and sea horses, among other delicacies.*
Opposite *An interesting barbeque stall in Wangfujing night market.*

食品名称	单位	单价
牛肉.羊肉.板筋 Yang/Niu rou/ Ban jiu	串	5元
炸臭豆腐 Fried-aroma bean-curd	串	4元
鸡肉.鸡心.鸡肫.小鸡仔 Ji rou/ji xin/ji zhen/x180js?	串	5元
炸蚕蛹 Fried silk-worm	串	5元
尤鱼头.海螺.田鸡.鱼皮 You yu tou/Hai luo/Tian ji/Yu pi	串	10元
炸大虾.鳝鱼.羊腰.豆皮 Zha da xia/Niu yu/Yang yao/Dou Bao	串	15元
海南椰子 Coconut	个	10-15元
糖葫芦 Crab apple bunch	串	5-10元

京族工商个体饮字 1193

Above *These farmers with their donkey were toiling in the fields beside the Great Wall.*

Beef in black bean sauce

750 g / 1 lb 10 oz rump steak, fat
   trimmed off
1 tablespoon canned black beans
1 teaspoon caster sugar
4 shallots, peeled and cut into large
   pieces
1 green pepper, deseeded and cut into
   2.5 cm / 1 inch squares
130 g can sliced bamboo shoots, rinsed
   well and dried
1 teaspoon mild curry powder
150 ml / 5 fl oz water
vegetable oil, for stir-frying

for the marinade

1 egg white
2 tablespoons dark soy sauce
1 teaspoon cornflour
1 tablespoon rice wine, sake or dry sherry

1 Mix all the ingredients for the marinade in a bowl.

2 Cut the steak into thin strips, about 5 x 2.5 cm / 2 x 1 inches. Place the steak in the marinade and turn to coat the meat, then leave for about 30 minutes.

3 Meanwhile, put the black beans in a bowl of cold water and leave for about 15 minutes. Drain the beans and rinse well, then add the sugar and mash the beans with a fork.

4 Heat a wok, add a little oil and stir-fry the shallots, green pepper, bamboo shoots and curry powder for about 2 minutes. Remove and put to one side.

5 Remove the beef from the marinade and, using the same oil, stir-fry the meat until browned. Save the marinade.

6 Add the vegetables, black beans, reserved marinade and the water to the beef, bring to the boil and stir until the sauce thickens. Serve at once.

Quick-fried beef with spinach

500 g / 1 lb 2 oz piece fillet steak,
    membrane trimmed off
5 cm / 2 inch piece fresh root ginger,
    peeled and cut into very thin slices
100 ml / 3½ fl oz fresh chicken stock
    (or use ½ stock cube dissolved in
    the same amount of water)
2 bags of baby spinach leaves,
    washed and dried
vegetable oil, for stir-frying

for the marinade
2 tablespoons dark soy sauce
2 or 3 tablespoons rice wine, sake or
    dry sherry
1 tsp sugar
½ tsp cornflour mixed with a little cold
    water to the consistency of single
    cream
a dash of sesame oil

1 Place the fillet steak in the freezer for 1 hour as this will make it easier to slice. Meanwhile, mix all the ingredients for the marinade in a bowl.

2 Remove the beef from the freezer and cut into wafer-thin slices – once sliced it will quickly defrost. Place the slices in the marinade and turn to coat the meat, then leave for 1 hour.

3 Heat a wok, add a little vegetable oil and stir-fry the ginger so that it is cooked but not brown, then remove from the wok and put to one side.

4 Heat some more oil in the wok until very hot, then stir-fry the meat in small batches until cooked rare – about 1 minute for each batch. Save the marinade.

5 Remove the meat from the wok and put to one side. Wipe out the wok, then add the marinade and chicken stock and heat until the mixture begins to boil.

6 Return the beef and ginger to the wok, add the spinach and stir-fry quickly until the spinach has wilted. Serve at once.

Right *The Chinese love to smoke.*

Stir-fried beef with Ginger sauce dip

1 quantity Ginger sauce (see page 181)

500 g / 1 lb 2 oz sirloin steak, fat trimmed off, and cut into 1 cm / ½ inch thick slices

vegetable oil, for deep-frying

for the marinade

2 tablespoons dark soy sauce

2 tablespoons light soy sauce

2.5 cm / 1 inch piece fresh root ginger, peeled and finely grated

a good pinch of sea salt

1 teaspoon caster sugar

¼ teaspoon chilli paste

1 large garlic clove, peeled and finely chopped

1 egg white

1 tablespoon cornflour

1 First prepare the Ginger sauce – you can do this at any time and keep it in the fridge until you get round to cooking the beef. Combine all the ingredients for the marinade in a bowl.

2 Cut the beef slices into 5 cm / 2 inch long strips, place in the marinade and turn to coat the meat, then leave for at least 30 minutes.

3 Heat sufficient oil for deep-frying in a wok until it is smoking hot. Remove the meat from the marinade and deep-fry until golden brown and cooked. Using a slotted spoon, remove the meat from the oil and drain on kitchen paper, then keep warm.

4 Heat up the Ginger sauce in a saucepan, pour into individual dipping dishes and serve with the beef.

Opposite top to bottom *Shandong-style pancakes make quick and tasty street food; having a break from Mr Jing's red taxi.* **Below** *Cooks at work in the kitchen of the Crowne Plaza Hotel, Beijing.*

Stir-fried beef with peanut (saté) sauce

500 g / 1 lb 2 oz piece fillet steak,
    membrane trimmed off
vegetable oil

for the marinade
150 ml / 5 fl oz soy sauce
2 or 3 teaspoons sesame oil
1 teaspoon cornflour
2 or 3 tablespoons water mixed with
    1 tablespoon vegetable oil

for the peanut sauce
1 medium onion, peeled and finely
    chopped
1 fat garlic clove, peeled and very finely
    chopped
1 tablespoon peanut (saté) sauce
a dash of rice wine, sake or dry sherry
1 teaspoon caster sugar
1 teaspoon mild curry powder
2 tablespoons water
2 tablespoons dark soy sauce
sea salt and freshly ground black pepper
    (optional)

1 Place the fillet of beef in the freezer for 1 hour as this will make it easier to slice. Meanwhile, mix all the ingredients for the marinade in a bowl.

2 Remove the beef from the freezer and slice the beef into wafer-thin slices. Place the slices in the marinade and turn to coat the meat, then leave for 1 hour.

3 Meanwhile, to make the peanut sauce, heat a little oil in a small frying pan and fry the onion and garlic until the onion is transparent. Stir in all the remaining sauce ingredients and bring gently to the boil, stirring all the time. Taste the sauce and maybe add a little salt and pepper or more soy sauce according to taste. Put the sauce to one side.

4 Heat a wok, add a little vegetable oil and brown the meat on both sides for a minute or two. If you have a small wok do the meat in batches. When the beef is cooked, stir in the sauce and heat through, then serve.

Below *Peanuts.* **Opposite** *A grocery store in Yongning.*

Pork

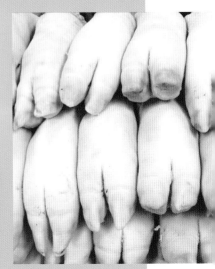

Above left to right *Garlic and chilli dipping sauce (page 114); having a breather in the countryside; these piggy trotters went to market.*

Pork

Pork is enormously popular in China and the many recipes for it range from simple, everyday dishes to more elaborate ones for celebrations.

The Chinese also like the fatty cuts of pork that we in the West disparage, but this is because their methods of cooking – simmering, slow cooking and braising – infuse the fat with the flavours of the dish and render it to a smooth and succulent texture.

Mild in flavour, pork is inherently versatile and can be successfully combined with many other textures and flavours. The Belly of pork with black bean and garlic sauce on page 111 is a full-bodied little number and would go well with either plain steamed rice or noodles to soak up the delicious sauce, while Red roast Chinese pork (page 114) couldn't be easier to make and will definitely impress.

Below *The kitchen of a small restaurant in the mountains. The owner is a farmer who decided to convert his business.*

Sweet and sour pork

1.25 kg / 2½ lb lean pork chops, boned
    and fat trimmed off
a little cornflour, to coat the meat
vegetable oil, for frying

for the marinade
2 teaspoons soft brown sugar
1 egg yolk
dark soy sauce
rice wine, sake or dry sherry

for the sauce
1 red pepper, deseeded and pith
    removed, cut into 4 pieces lengthways
1 cucumber, peeled, halved lengthways
    and deseeded
2 stringed celery sticks, trimmed of the
    green leaves
2 tablespoons tomato sauce
150 ml / 5 fl oz white rice vinegar
200 ml / 7 fl oz chicken stock (or use
    ½ stock cube dissolved in the same
    amount of water)
1 heaped tablespoon cornflour mixed
    with a little cold water to the
    consistency of single cream
1 large onion, peeled and cut into 1 cm /
    ½ inch chunks
125 g / 4½ oz button mushrooms, cut into
    quarters
400 g / 14 oz fresh pineapple, peeled and
    cut into 2.5 cm / 1 inch batons

1 Cut the chops into 2.5 cm / 1 inch cubes and put into a bowl.

2 To make the marinade, mix the sugar and egg yolk with enough soy sauce and wine, sake or sherry in equal quantities to cover the meat, then leave for 1 hour.

3 Meanwhile, start preparing the sauce. Cut each red pepper strip into 2.5 cm / 1 inch long diamond shapes. Slice each cucumber half lengthways on the diagonal into pieces about 3.5 cm / 1½ inches long. Cut the celery sticks on the diagonal into pieces 2.5 cm / 1 inch long.

4 Mix the tomato sauce with the rice vinegar and stock, then stir in the cornflour mixture and put to one side.

5 Drain the meat from the marinade, reserving the liquid, and toss the meat lightly in a little cornflour.

6 Heat a wok, add some oil and stir-fry the pork in batches until golden brown and cooked through – 7 or 8 minutes. Drain on kitchen paper and put to one side.

7 Stir-fry the onion, celery and red pepper in hot oil for about 1 minute, add the mushrooms and cook for 1 minute, then add the pineapple and cook for 1 minute. Finally, add the cucumber and stir-fry for another minute or so.

8 Stir in the tomato sauce mixture and the reserved marinade and bubble until the sauce thickens nicely. Add the pork pieces to the sauce to heat through, then serve.

Opposite *This meat section of the market wasn't for the faint-hearted.*

Belly of pork with black bean and garlic sauce

750 g / 1 lb 10 oz belly of pork, cut into
1 cm / ½ inch strips, skin, but not fat,
removed
vegetable oil, for frying

for the sauce
2 or 3 tablespoons canned black beans,
rinsed and drained
200 ml / 7 fl oz water
2 or 3 teaspoons dark soy sauce
2.5 cm / 1 inch piece fresh root ginger,
peeled and finely grated
3 fat garlic cloves, peeled and finely
grated

a little added extra!
2 tablespoons cornflour mixed with a little
cold water to the consistency of single
cream
a good dash of rice wine, sake or dry
sherry

1 Cut the pork strips into 5 cm / 2 inch pieces.

2 To make the sauce, put the black beans in a blender
with the water and whiz to a purée. Mix the purée with
the soy sauce, ginger and garlic.

3 Heat a little oil in a pan and stir-fry the pork pieces
until golden brown and slightly crispy.

4 Add the sauce mixture to the pork, cover and simmer
for about 1 hour. Check from time to time that the sauce
is not too dry and, if necessary, add a little hot water.

5 When the meat is cooked, stir in the little added
extras and keep stirring until the sauce boils and
thickens, then serve.

Opposite *Garlic*. **Below** *No pre-packaged stuff here.*

Opposite *A rose between two racks of ribs.* **Above** *Country folk enjoying the sun.*

Barbeque-style pork spare ribs

1 kg / 2¼ lb rack of pork spare ribs

for the marinade

4 tablespoons barbeque sauce

4 tablespoons runny honey

4 tablespoons malt vinegar

4 tablespoons rice wine, sake or dry
sherry

1 tablespoon chilli sauce

¼ teaspoon five-spice powder (see
page 178)

2 tablespoons dark soy sauce

1 very fat garlic clove, peeled and finely
grated

2.5 cm / 1 inch piece fresh root ginger,
peeled and finely grated

a little added extra!

Make up about 200 ml / 7 fl oz chicken
stock and add a couple of dashes of
soy sauce

1 Mix all the ingredients for the marinade in a bowl. Place the rack of ribs in a shallow roasting tin and coat with the marinade, then leave for at least 1½ hours, turning them at least twice during that time to allow the ribs to fully absorb the marinade.

2 Preheat the oven to 200°C / 400°F / gas mark 6. Pour off any excess marinade and reserve, then cook the ribs, basting frequently, for about 1 hour or until the pork is tender.

3 Lift the roasting tin onto the top of the stove and transfer the pork ribs to a chopping board. Stir the chicken stock and soy mixture and any reserved marinade into the juices left in the roasting tin and cook over a low heat for about 5 minutes, whisking continuously.

4 Chop the rack into individual ribs, place on a serving dish and pour over the juices from the roasting tin. Serve with a side dish of Chinese pickles (see page 186) or buy a jar of pickles from your Chinese supermarket.

Red roast Chinese pork

600 g / 1 lb 5 oz piece fillet of pork, membrane trimmed off

for the marinade

5 tablespoons light soy sauce
1 teaspoon five-spice powder (see page 178)
2 tablespoons soft brown sugar
1 heaped teaspoon natural Chinese red colouring powder

for the dipping sauce

2 garlic cloves, peeled and minced
3 or 4 red chillies, very finely sliced lengthways (deseeded if you like)
½ wine glass red Chinese vinegar

1 Mix all the ingredients for the marinade in a dish. Add the pork and turn to coat thoroughly, then leave in the fridge overnight.

2 If you are fortunate enough to have a rotisserie in your oven, thread the loin of pork onto the skewer and roast at about 200°C/400°F/gas mark 6 for 20–30 minutes. Baste with the rest of the marinade from time to time. If you don't have a rotisserie, lay the pork on a griddle in a roasting pan and turn from time to time to evenly cook the fillet on all sides. Check that the pork is cooked, then remove from the oven and leave to rest in a warm place for 10 minutes.

3 Meanwhile, mix all the ingredients for the dipping sauce.

4 Carve the pork into thin slices and serve each helping with a very tiny bowl of the dipping sauce. Rice and steamed vegetables would go well with this dish.

Slow-simmered pork casserole

750 g / 1 lb 10 oz piece lean loin of pork,
    membrane trimmed off

2 or 3 tablespoons rice wine, sake or dry
    sherry

6 tablespoons dark soy sauce

2 x 2.5 cm / 1 inch piece fresh root
    ginger, peeled and finely chopped

2 or 3 spring onions, trimmed and
    coarsely chopped

2 tablespoons soft brown sugar

1 Plunge the pork into boiling water and blanch for 2 minutes. Remove the pork and save the water. Rinse the pork in cold water, pat dry and cut into 5 cm / 2 inch cubes.

2 Put the pork in a heavy-based casserole, with a lid, and pour in enough of the reserved blanching water to just cover the meat (discard the rest).

3 Bring to the boil, then reduce the heat and add the rice wine, sake or sherry, the soy sauce, ginger and spring onions. Cover the pan and simmer very gently for about 2 hours, stirring from time to time.

4 Check that the meat is tender, then add the sugar, bring to the boil and stir until the sauce coats the meat.

Below *This young lady was rather suspicious of the camera, unlike the gentleman to her left.*

Above *A chance to enjoy a drink at the trendy No Name bar in the lakes area of Houhai District, Beijing.*

Pork with black bean sauce

400 g / 14 oz loin of pork, membrane and
   sinew trimmed off
plain flour, to coat the meat
1 small red pepper and 1 small green
   pepper, each deseeded and pith
   removed, then cut into 1 cm / ½ inch
   squares
1 fat garlic clove, peeled and finely
   chopped
2.5 cm / 1 inch piece fresh root ginger,
   peeled and finely chopped
4 or 5 spring onions, trimmed and sliced
   diagonally into 2.5 cm / 1 inch lengths
3 tablespoons black bean sauce
a dash of rice wine, sake or dry sherry
sea salt
vegetable oil, for stir-frying
a few drops of sesame oil, to finish

1 Cut the pork into 1 cm / ½ inch thick medallions. Lightly coat with flour and beat out to flatten into escalopes.

2 Heat a wok, add a little vegetable oil and stir-fry the peppers for 1–2 minutes.

3 Add the garlic, ginger, spring onions, a good pinch of salt and the pork escalopes and stir-fry for 2–3 minutes.

4 Add the black bean sauce and the rice wine, sake or sherry and mix until well blended and heated through.

5 Transfer to a warm dish, sprinkle over a few drops of sesame oil and serve.

Chinese pork and peppers

500 g / 1 lb 2 oz loin of pork, membrane
    trimmed off
1 red pepper and 1 green pepper, each
    cut into quarters lengthways,
    deseeded and pith removed
1 large onion, peeled and chopped into
    1 cm / ½ inch pieces
1 fat garlic clove, peeled and finely
    chopped
150 g / 5 oz button mushrooms, chopped
2.5 cm / 1 inch piece fresh root ginger,
    peeled and finely chopped
¼ teaspoon hot red chilli flakes
3 or 4 tablespoons rice wine, sake or dry
    sherry
1 tablespoon dark soy sauce
150 ml / 5 fl oz chicken stock
1 tablespoon cornflour mixed with a little
    cold water to the consistency of single
    cream
vegetable oil, for stir-frying

1 Cut the pork into 5–7.5 cm / 2–3 inch long strips
1 cm / ½ inch wide. Cut the pepper quarters into thin
slices the same size as the pork.

2 Heat a wok, add a little oil and stir-fry the onion
until soft, then add the garlic and stir-fry for about
30 seconds.

3 Add the pork and stir-fry for 4–5 minutes until it is
browned on both sides and cooked through. Remove the
pork from the wok and put to one side in a warm place.

4 Add the mushrooms, ginger, pepper slices, chilli
flakes, rice wine, sake or sherry and the soy sauce to the
wok and stir-fry until the mushrooms soften.

5 Add the stock and cornflour mixture and stir until the
sauce begins to thicken.

6 Return the pork to the wok and serve piping hot.

Right *A rather magnificent Buddhist statue.*
Opposite *Having a tasty pancake snack in the
Julong Gardens. Mr Jing finds it rather amusing.*

Party
Food

Above left to right *Mrs Li fries some stuffing for dumplings (page 127); a countryside meal – dumplings, herbs with tofu and salad of wild herbs; outdoor kitchens in Beijing's Tuanjiehu District.*

Party food

What I have called party food really should be called 'delicious snacks'. If you make three or four of any of these recipes, you are effectively making the equivalent of European canapés delicious food to be enjoyed in a light hearted way, especially in the summertime, when the weather is fine and you are having a few drinks with friends, rather than sitting down to a formal feast.

We're all familiar with spring rolls and dumplings – and jolly popular they are, too. But it's easy to make your own and you can experiment with your favourite stuffings. When I visited Mrs Sun, she and a neighbour (that's them below with Mr Jing) rustled up a mountain of dumplings in no time at all.

Serve all these recipes with a selection of dips (see page 175).

Below *Mr Jing rolls the dough while the women stuff dumplings with the fillings.*

Deep-fried chicken and seaweed rolls

200 g / 7 oz skinless, boneless chicken breast, finely minced with

75 g / 3 oz fatty pork, such as belly of pork

6 water chestnuts, rinsed, dried and minced

2 tablespoons sesame oil

1 tablespoon cornflour

a dash of light soy sauce

1 thin slice peeled fresh root ginger, minced

6 sheets lava seaweed, layered in wet cloths for 10 minutes before using

a little flour and water paste, to seal the rolls

100 g / 3½ oz toasted white sesame seeds

sea salt and freshly ground black pepper

vegetable oil, for deep-frying

1 Combine the minced chicken and pork with the water chestnuts, sesame oil and cornflour. Season with soy sauce, salt and pepper.

2 Cut the seaweed into 3.5 cm / 1½ inch wide strips. Place about 1 tablespoon of the chicken mixture on each strip of seaweed and roll up, then tuck in the edges and seal the end with a little flour and water paste. Dip the ends of each roll into the sesame seeds.

3 Heat a wok, add enough vegetable oil for deep-frying and, when hot, fry the rolls for 3–4 minutes. Drain on kitchen paper and serve with a selection of dips (see page 175).

Below *Mahjiang players enjoy a game in the street.* **Opposite** *The chefs in the steamy heat of the Crowne Plaza Hotel, Beijing.*

Above left to right *Small portions of dough that will be turned into dumplings; onion and cabbage are used for the stuffing in Mrs Li's kitchen; dumplings ready for steaming.*

Dumpling wrappers

You can, in fact, buy dumpling wrappers if you are lucky enough to have a stockist near you. However, they are very easy to make yourself and below is a good straightforward recipe. Bean curd skins also work as dumpling wrappers, but they are quite fragile and brittle so layer the skins in damp cloths to reconstitute them before using.

Makes about 20

350 g / 8 oz plain flour, plus extra for
    dusting
1 teaspoon baking powder
1 teaspoon sea salt
2 eggs, separated
140 ml / 4½ fl oz warm water

1 Sift all the dry ingredients into a bowl.

2 Beat the egg yolks with the water.

3 Make a well in the centre of the dry ingredients and pour in the egg and water mixture. Mix to a dough with a fork, then dive in with your hands and transfer the dough to a well-floured surface and knead well for about 4 minutes. Roll the dough in flour and wrap in clingfilm for about 10 minutes.

4 Roll out the dough to a strip about 2.5 mm / ⅛ inch thick and, using a pastry cutter, cut into 8.5 cm / 3½ inch circles. Fill as desired (see opposite), then fold and use egg white to seal the edges.

Stuffing for dumplings

Fills 20 wrappers

Pork and vegetable

300 g / 11 oz finely minced fillet of pork

300 g / 11 oz blanched Chinese cabbage leaves, cooled, very finely chopped and any excess moisture squeezed out

1 thin slice peeled fresh root ginger, very finely minced

2 garlic cloves, peeled and very finely minced

2 spring onions, trimmed and minced

4 tablespoons water

1 tablespoon sesame oil

a dash of rice wine, sake or dry sherry

1 teaspoon caster sugar

a pinch each of sea salt and freshly ground black pepper

1 teaspoon light soy sauce

cabbage leaves, for steaming

1 Mix all the ingredients except the whole cabbage leaves in a bowl and put in the fridge for at least 1 hour.

2 Place a heaped teaspoon of the filling in the centre of each dumpling wrapper, then fold the wrapper over into a half moon shape, paint the edges with egg white and press firmly to seal.

3 Line a bamboo steamer with cabbage leaves, lay the dumplings on the leaves and steam with the lid on for 10–12 minutes, then serve with a selection of dips (see page 175).

Prawn

300 g / 11 oz large shelled raw prawns, deveined and very finely chopped

1 egg white, lightly beaten

2 spring onions, trimmed and minced

2 tablespoons finely diced bamboo shoots

2 tablespoons finely minced pork fat

2 tablespoons light soy sauce

1 tablespoon cornflour

1 thin slice peeled fresh root ginger, very finely minced

a dash of rice wine, sake or dry sherry

a pinch each of sea salt and freshly ground black pepper

cabbage leaves, for steaming

1 Prepare and cook as in Pork and vegetable above.

(more luscious stuffings on the next page)

Stuffing for dumplings *(continued)*

Pork and seafood

150 g / 5 oz finely minced fillet of pork
150 g / 5 oz large shelled raw prawns, deveined
    and finely chopped
50 g / 2 oz diced raw scallop or crab meat
3 spring onions, trimmed and finely chopped
2 thin slices peeled fresh root ginger, very finely
    minced
2 tablespoons sesame oil

1 tablespoon soy sauce
a dash of rice wine, sake or dry sherry
a pinch each of sea salt and freshly ground black
    pepper
cabbage leaves, for steaming

1 Prepare and cook as for Pork and vegetable on
page 127.

Vegetable

40 g / 1½ oz Chinese black mushrooms,
    reconstituted in a little warm water for
    30 minutes, stalks discarded, then finely
    chopped
300 g / 11 oz fresh bamboo shoots, parboiled in
    boiling salted water for 5 minutes, then
    drained and finely chopped
1 small block of firm bean curd, very finely
    chopped
300 g / 11 oz blanched Chinese cabbage leaves,
    cooled, very finely chopped and any excess
    moisture squeezed out
a pinch each of sea salt and freshly ground black
    pepper
sesame oil, for stir-frying
cabbage leaves, for steaming

1 Heat a wok, add a little oil and stir-fry the
mushrooms, bamboo shoots and bean curd for
2–3 minutes. Season with salt and pepper and
allow to cool.

2 Mix in the chopped cabbage, then stuff and
cook the dumplings as for Pork and vegetable on
page 127.

*Below My good friend Mrs Sun prefers to boil her
dumplings. Opposite Dumplings ready for the pot.*

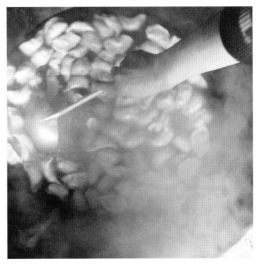

Shrimp toast

300 g/11 oz peeled shrimps or small
    shelled raw prawns, finely minced with
75 g/3 oz fatty pork, such as belly of
    pork
6 water chestnuts, rinsed, dried and
    minced
2 spring onions, trimmed and minced
1 egg white, beaten
2 teaspoons cornflour
1 tablespoon sesame oil
a dash of rice wine, sake or dry sherry
6 slices white bread, crusts removed
2 tablespoons minced cooked ham
3 tablespoons white sesame seeds
sea salt and freshly ground black pepper
vegetable oil, for frying

1 Mix the minced shrimps or prawns and the pork with the water chestnuts, spring onions, egg white, cornflour and sesame oil. Season with rice wine, sake or sherry and salt and pepper and beat to a paste.

2 Spread the mixture over the bread, then sprinkle with the ham and sesame seeds, pressing them lightly into the paste. Cut each slice into three strips.

3 Shallow-fry the strips on each side in vegetable oil until golden, then drain on kitchen paper and serve.

Below *A grocery shop in Yongning District.* **Opposite** *A very happy Buddha in the White Cloud Taoist Temple.*

Above *Meeting and greeting in the hotel's restaurant.*

Spring roll wrappers

You can buy these wrappers in some of the larger supermarkets or in Asian stores. However, they are very easy to make yourself and below is a good straightforward recipe.

Makes about 50

1.5 kg / 3½ lb plain flour
1½ teaspoons sea salt
750 ml / 1¼ pints water
a little vegetable oil

1 Sift the flour and salt into a bowl. Gradually add the water, stirring with a fork until you have a soft and sticky dough, then cover with clingfilm and leave for 1 hour.

2 Knead the dough for 3–4 minutes.

3 Heat a very lightly oiled pan or griddle on a medium heat until the surface of the pan is medium hot. Rub the dough over the surface of the pan so that a very thin layer sticks to the pan.

4 When the edges of the dough start to curl, remove from the pan and stack ready for use. Repeat with the remaining dough.

Pork, beansprout and mushroom spring rolls

Makes 10

175 g/6 oz lean pork or chicken,
   shredded
25 g/1 oz pork or bacon fat, shredded
60 g/2½ oz bamboo shoots, rinsed,
   dried and shredded
250 g/9 oz beansprouts
2 or 3 spring onions, trimmed and
   shredded
2 Chinese dried black mushrooms,
   reconstituted in a little warm water for
   30 minutes, stalks discarded, then
   finely chopped
1½ tablespoons light soy sauce
1 teaspoon caster sugar
2 teaspoons cornflour mixed with a little
   cold water to the consistency of single
   cream
10 spring roll wrappers (see opposite)
sea salt and freshly ground black pepper
vegetable oil, for frying

1 Heat a wok, add some oil and stir-fry the pork or chicken with the pork or bacon fat for a minute or so.

2 Add the vegetables and stir-fry for about 30 seconds, then season with the soy sauce, sugar, salt and pepper and stir-fry for about 30 seconds.

3 Add the cornflour mixture and cook, stirring well, until the mixture thickens slightly.

4 Place a little filling in the middle of each spring roll wrapper and roll up, tucking the ends in, then seal the edges with water.

5 Heat enough oil for deep-frying in a wok and, when hot, fry the spring rolls until golden brown. Remove from the wok and drain on kitchen paper, then serve with your favourite dip (see page 175).

Right *A pancake production line in a market near Julong Gardens.*

Steamed beef balls

500 g / 1 lb 2 oz rump or sirloin steak, fat
    trimmed off, finely minced with
150 g / 5 oz fatty pork, such as belly of
    pork
6 spring onions, trimmed and finely
    chopped
same quantity of freshly chopped
    coriander leaves (will depend on the
    size of your spring onions)
2 egg whites, well beaten
cabbage leaves, for steaming

for the marinade
2 or 3 pieces dried tangerine or orange
    peel (from Asian stores), softened in a
    little warm water
1 teaspoon baking powder
2 tablespoons oyster sauce
4 teaspoons caster sugar
a pinch of sea salt

1 Combine all the ingredients for the marinade in a bowl, add the minced beef and pork and turn to coat the meat, then marinate in the fridge for at least 1 hour.

2 Add the spring onions and coriander and stir to mix thoroughly, then stir in the egg white.

3 Form the mixture into little balls about 2.5 cm / 1 inch round.

4 Line a bamboo steamer with the cabbage leaves, place the balls on the leaves and steam over a pan of boiling water, with the lid on, for 8–10 minutes. Serve with a variety of dipping sauces (see page 176).

Below *Dried orange peel.* Opposite *The hospitable Mr Yang and Mrs Li in their simple home.*

Noodles and Rice

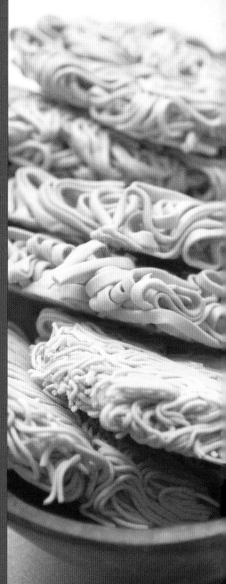

Above left to right *Chefs preparing noodles at a restaurant in Houhai; halfway through a bowl of very good noodles from Old Beijing Zhajiang Noodle King; kneading the noodle dough.*

Noodles and Rice

With Italian pasta, you know that you have the wide strips of tagliatelle and you have the thin, rounded spaghetti style of pasta. However, in China they also make noodles from rice flour, not just wheat flour, so the rice flour noodles, often referred to as glass noodles, are very fine and not dissimilar to Italian vermicelli. The rice noodles are particularly good in soups and hotpots, but for the trencherman, the big, flat, wheat noodles will appease the most hungry appetite. In my view, for making fried noodle dishes you should use the thin egg and wheat noodles. The thick noodles work terribly well in sumptuous bowls of noodle soup, while the thin ones, crisply fried, are more refined and gastronomically elegant.

When you are using noodles in soup, whether they are thick or thin, cook them first in boiling salted water as per instructions on the packet, then drain, rinse and leave them to cool. You can then put your noodles into the serving bowl first and the addition of the hot liquid poured on will heat them up perfectly. This saves a lot of time.

Below *Stretching the dough for noodles by hand.*

Fish noodle soup

450 g / 1 lb monkfish or other firm-
    fleshed white fish, skinned and cut
    into 2.5 cm / 1 inch cubes
1.5 litres / 2½ pints fish stock
150 g / 5 oz broccoli stalks, peeled and
    cut into batons 3.5 cm / 1½ inches
    long by 1 cm / ½ inch thick
15 g / ½ oz Chinese dried black
    mushrooms, reconstituted in a little
    warm water for 30 minutes, stalks
    discarded, then diced
150 g / 5 oz shelled small raw prawns
150 g / 5 oz Chinese cabbage leaves,
    coarsely chopped
1 tablespoon cornflour mixed with a little
    cold water to the consistency of single
    cream
800 g / 1 lb 12 oz boiled plain noodles
vegetable oil, for stir-frying

for the marinade

1 egg white, beaten until frothy
1 teaspoon cornflour
a pinch each of sea salt and white
    pepper
a dash of rice wine, sake or dry sherry

for the soup base

1 tablespoon soy bean paste
½ teaspoon sea salt
a good dash of malt vinegar
a pinch of freshly ground black pepper
1 teaspoon minced, peeled fresh root
    ginger

for the garnish

200 g / 7 oz finely chopped pickled
    mustard greens
5 tablespoons finely chopped spring
    onions

1 Mix all the ingredients for the marinade in a bowl, add the monkfish, stir well to coat the fish and leave in the fridge for 30 minutes.

2 Meanwhile, combine all the ingredients for the soup base. Heat a wok, add a little oil, then add the soup base mixture and stir-fry for a minute or two. Pour in the stock and bring to the boil, then reduce the heat and simmer, uncovered, for 30 minutes.

3 Meanwhile, separately blanch both the broccoli stalks and diced mushrooms in boiling salted water for 1 minute, then drain.

4 Add the broccoli stalks to the wok, then a minute later add the mushroom, prawns and Chinese leaves and simmer for 10–15 minutes.

5 Add the monkfish and simmer for 5 minutes.

6 Add the cornflour mixture and stir until the soup thickens.

7 Place the cooked noodles in individual bowls (see page 139) and top with the pickled mustard greens and spring onions. Pour the soup over the noodles and serve.

Below *Old Beijing Zhajiang Noodle King restaurant.*

Delicate string noodle soup

200 g / 7 oz fillet of pork, membrane
   trimmed off, then cut into very fine
   strips
5 or 6 spring onions, trimmed and sliced
   diagonally into 2.5 cm / 1 inch lengths
50 g / 2 oz dried baby shrimps, rinsed
   and softened in warm water
15 g / ½ oz Chinese dried black
   mushrooms, reconstituted in a little
   warm water for 30 minutes, stalks
   discarded, then diced
1 litre / 1¾ pints chicken stock
a dash of sesame oil
250 g / 9 oz Chinese cabbage, coarsely
   chopped
800 g / 1 lb 12 oz boiled rice string
   noodles
a pinch of sea salt
white pepper
vegetable oil, for stir-frying

for the marinade
1 tablespoon cornflour
1 teaspoon sesame oil
1 teaspoon soy sauce
a good dash of rice wine, sake or dry
   sherry
a pinch of sea salt

for the garnish
200 g / 7 oz finely chopped pickled
   mustard greens
5 tablespoons very finely chopped spring
   onions

Above *Rice noodles.*

1 Mix all the ingredients for the marinade in a bowl, add the pork, stir well to coat the meat, then leave in the fridge for 30 minutes.

2 Heat a wok, add a little vegetable oil and stir-fry the spring onions and shrimps for a minute or two.

3 Stir in the mushrooms and stir-fry for 1 minute.

4 Add the pork strips and stir-fry for 3 or 4 minutes, or until cooked.

5 Add the stock, sesame oil, salt and pepper and bring to the boil.

6 Add the cabbage and stir for 3–5 minutes or until the cabbage is just cooked, but with a little bite.

7 Place the cooked noodles in individual bowls and top with the mustard greens and spring onions. Pour the soup over the noodles and serve.

Fillet of beef noodle soup

1 small red shallot or ½ red onion, peeled
   and finely minced
2 fat garlic cloves, peeled and minced
400 g / 14 oz fillet steak, trimmed and cut
   into 5 x 1 cm / 2 x ½ inch strips
200 g / 7 oz sliced bamboo shoots, rinsed
   and dried
1 medium carrot, peeled and cut into
   thin slices, blanched briefly in boiling
   water and drained
185 g / 6½ oz bean curd, cut into slices
   about 2.5 x 5 cm / 1 x 2 inch (use
   white yam cake if you can find it – if
   you use yam cake, score the slices
   slightly)
1 litre / 1¾ pints hot beef stock
185 g / 6½ oz baby bok choi, cut
   lengthways into quarters
800 g / 1 lb 12 oz boiled plain noodles
vegetable oil, for frying

for the soup base
3 or 4 spring onions, trimmed and sliced
   diagonally into 2.5 cm / 1 inch lengths
2 thin slices peeled fresh root ginger, cut
   into very thin strips
4 tablespoons dark soy sauce
2 tablespoons soybean paste
1 tablespoon hot soybean paste
1 tablespoon sesame oil
2 tablespoons red Chinese vinegar
1 teaspoon caster sugar
a pinch of white pepper

1 Heat a wok, add a little vegetable oil and stir-fry the shallot or onion and the garlic until soft.

2 Add the beef strips, bamboo shoots and carrot and cook for 4–5 minutes.

3 Add the bean curd and stir-fry the mixture gently for 1–2 minutes.

4 Mix the ingredients for the soup base in a bowl, then add to the wok and stir-fry for a couple of minutes.

5 Pour the stock into the wok and bring to the boil, then add the bok choi, reduce the heat and cook for a further 5–10 minutes.

6 Place the cooked noodles in individual bowls, pour the soup over the noodles and serve.

Below *Two cooks snatch a few free minutes before their shift begins.* Opposite *At a restaurant in Houhai District, a woman enjoys her bowl of noodles.*

Noodle soup with garlic spare ribs

It is most important in this dish to get a rack or two of baby pork ribs; therefore you may have to order them in advance from your friendly butcher.

about 400 g / 14 oz baby pork ribs,
　　chopped into 2.5 cm / 1 inch square
　　pieces
5 fat garlic cloves, peeled and minced
1 litre/ 1¾ pints chicken stock
1 tablespoon soy sauce
1 teaspoon sesame oil
a pinch each of sea salt and freshly
　　ground black pepper
250 g / 9 oz bok choi, cut into pieces
　　about 2.5 cm / 1 inch long
800 g / 1 lb 12 oz boiled plain noodles
vegetable oil, for stir-frying
chopped spring onions, to garnish

for the marinade

1 egg white, beaten
1 tablespoon cornflour
2 garlic cloves, peeled and minced
2.5 cm / 1 inch piece fresh root ginger,
　　peeled and minced
a good dash of dark soy sauce
a couple of dashes of sesame oil
a pinch of white pepper
a little rice wine, sake or dry sherry

for the soup base

2 tablespoons dark soy sauce
2 tablespoons rice wine, sake or dry
　　sherry
225 ml / 8 fl oz chicken stock
1 tablespoon brown sugar crystals
a pinch of white pepper
a pinch of five-spice powder (see page
　　178)

Above *My turn to serve the noodles.*

1 Mix all the ingredients for the marinade in a bowl. Add the pork, stir well to coat the meat, then leave in the fridge for 30–40 minutes.

2 Heat a wok, add some vegetable oil and stir-fry the garlic until soft.

3 Add the pork and stir until coated with the oil and garlic, then add all the ingredients for the soup base and bring to the boil. Reduce the heat to low and simmer for about 30 minutes, turning the pork every 10 minutes or so.

4 When the pork is very tender, remove from the wok and transfer to a plate. Add the stock, soy sauce, sesame oil and seasoning to the juices in the wok and bring to the boil.

5 Add the bok choi and simmer until cooked.

6 Place the cooked noodles in a large serving bowl, arrange the pork on top, pour over the soup and garnish with the spring onions.

Noodle soup with beef saté

1 dessertspoon cornflour

300 g / 11 oz fillet steak, trimmed and cut into thin strips, about 2.5 cm / 1 inch long

1 red onion or shallot, peeled and finely chopped

2 red chillies, cut into thin rings (deseeded if you like)

2 fat garlic cloves, peeled and minced

3.5 cm / 1½ inch piece fresh root ginger, peeled and minced

1.5 litres / 2½ pints hot beef stock

200 g / 7 oz bok choi, cut into 2.5 cm / 1 inch pieces

800 g / 1 lb 12 oz boiled plain noodles

vegetable oil, for stir-frying

for the soup base

10 tablespoons peanut (saté) paste

6 tablespoons coconut cream

4 tablespoons sake, rice wine or dry sherry

4 tablespoons Chinese curry powder

4 tablespoons light soy sauce

2 tablespoons caster sugar

2 tablespoons oyster sauce

zest of ½ lemon

1 Mix the cornflour with a little vegetable oil to a smooth paste in a bowl, then add the beef strips, turn to coat in the mixture and marinate in the fridge for 1 hour.

2 Heat a wok, add a little oil and stir-fry the onion, chilli, garlic and ginger until soft.

3 Add the ingredients for the soup base and stir-fry until evenly mixed, then add the stock and bring to the boil.

4 Add the beef slices, reduce the heat and simmer for 5 minutes.

5 Add the bok choi and simmer until all the ingredients are cooked.

6 Place the cooked noodles in the bottom of a large serving bowl, pour the soup over and serve.

Right (left to right) *Thin, medium, thick noodles.*

Noodle pancakes

To make noodle pancakes, use thin egg noodles and prepare as on page 139. Then, simply heat enough vegetable oil for shallow-frying in a 12.5–15 cm/5–6 inch diameter pan until hot, take your cooked noodles and fry them on both sides until they are crispy. Drain on kitchen paper. As with the boiled noodles, when you later put the toppings on them they will heat the noodle pancakes through.

Noodle pancake with chicken and ham

500 g/1 lb 2 oz egg noodle pancake (see above)
250 g/9 oz skinless, boneless chicken breast, cut into strips the same size as the mangetout (below)
250 g/9 oz Chinese cabbage leaves, chopped to the same size as the mangetout
100 g/3½ oz stringed mangetout
150 g/5 oz slice good-quality cooked ham (off the bone), cut to the same size as the mangetout
vegetable oil, for stir-frying

for the marinade

2 tablespoons vegetable oil
1 egg white, beaten
1 tablespoon cornflour
2 tablespoons rice wine, sake or dry sherry
sea salt and freshly ground black pepper

for the soup base

675 ml/1 pint 3 fl oz chicken stock
2 tablespoons light soy sauce
2 tablespoons rice wine, sake or dry sherry
a pinch of sea salt
1 tablespoon cornflour mixed with a little cold water to the consistency of single cream

1 Make the noodle pancake and put to one side.

2 Mix all the ingredients for the marinade in a bowl, then add the chicken pieces, stir well to coat and leave in the fridge for 30–40 minutes.

3 Heat a wok, add some oil and stir-fry the chicken strips until golden brown, then drain and put to one side.

4 Add the cabbage and mangetout to the wok and stir-fry just to soften, then drain and put to one side.

5 Next, stir-fry the ham until it is slightly golden, then return the chicken, cabbage and mangetout to the wok.

6 Mix all the ingredients for the soup base in a bowl, then add to the wok and, stirring continuously, bring to the boil. Check the chicken is cooked.

7 Place the noodle pancake in a serving dish, pour over the chicken mixture and serve.

Opposite *A fried noodle pancake.* **Right** *Bicycle repair shops are plentiful in China.*

Stir-fried squid and pork on noodle pancake

500 g/1 lb 2 oz noodle pancake (see
    page 147)
100 g/3½ oz squid tubes, cleaned
100 g/3½ oz fillet of pork, membrane
    trimmed off and cut into thin slices
100 g/3½ oz shelled raw tiger prawns
    (tails left on), deveined (see page 71)
100 g/3½ oz stringed mangetout
vegetable oil, for stir-frying

for soup base
675 ml/1 pint 3 fl oz chicken stock
2 tablespoons light soy sauce
2 teaspoons cornflour
1 teaspoon caster sugar
1 teaspoon sesame oil
a pinch of sea salt

1 Make the noodle pancake and put to one side.

2 Cut open the squid tubes lengthways to form a flat
sheet and score the inside of the squid in a criss-cross
pattern. Cut the squid sheet into 2.5 cm/1 inch squares.

3 Heat a wok, add some vegetable oil and stir-fry the
pork for 4–5 minutes, then add the squid and cook for
30 seconds. Add the prawns and mangetout and stir fry
for about 1 minute until the prawns turn pink.

4 Stir in the ingredients for the soup base and bring to
the boil.

5 Place the noodle pancake in a serving dish, pour over
the squid and pork mixture and serve.

Deep-fried noodles with mixed seafood

500 g / 1 lb 2 oz egg noodle pancake (see page 147)

250 g / 9 oz skinned, firm fish fillet, such as cod or bass

150 g / 5 oz shelled raw tiger prawns, deveined (see page 71)

20 g / ¾ oz Chinese dried black mushrooms, reconstituted in a little warm water for 30 minutes, stalks discarded, then cut into strips

6 spring onions, trimmed and sliced diagonally into 2.5 cm / 1 inch lengths

4 thin slices peeled fresh root ginger, cut into very thin strips

250 g / 9 oz bok choi, chopped into 2.5 cm / 1 inch pieces

150 g / 5 oz bamboo shoots, thinly sliced

vegetable oil, for frying

for the marinade

3 tablespoons vegetable oil

sea salt and white pepper

for the soup base

450 ml / 15 fl oz fish stock

2 tablespoons light soy sauce

2 teaspoons cornflour

1 teaspoon caster sugar

a pinch of sea salt

1 Make the noodle pancake and put to one side.

2 Mix the ingredients for the marinade in a bowl. Score diagonal diamond slits on both surfaces of the fish fillet and cut into 2 x 3.5 cm / ¾ x 1½ inch pieces. Add the fish and prawns to the marinade and stir to coat, then leave in the fridge for 30 minutes.

3 Heat a wok, add a little oil and very lightly fry the fish and prawns until they start to colour but are not quite cooked, then remove from the pan and put to one side.

4 Now, stir-fry the mushrooms, spring onions and ginger in the same oil for 3–4 minutes.

5 Add the bok choi and bamboo shoots, stir together, then stir in all the ingredients for the soup base. Add the fish and prawns and bring to the boil.

6 Place the noodle pancake in a large serving bowl, pour over the seafood soup and serve.

Below *A realistic window display at the Old Beijing Zhajiang Noodle King restaurant.* Opposite *Mr Jing and I getting stuck into our noodles at the restaurant.*

Stir-fried fillet of beef with noodle pancake

500 g / 1 lb 2 oz egg noodle pancake (see page 147)

250 g / 9 oz fillet steak, trimmed and cut into thin strips

300 g / 11 oz broccoli stalks, peeled and cut into 5 cm / 2 inch batons

3 tablespoons peanut (saté) paste

3 fat garlic cloves, peeled and minced

vegetable oil, for frying

for the marinade

4 tablespoons water

2 tablespoons vegetable oil

1 tablespoon dark soy sauce

2 teaspoons cornflour

¼ teaspoon baking powder

¼ teaspoon white pepper

for the soup base

675 ml / 1 pint 3 fl oz beef stock

2 tablespoons light soy sauce

2 teaspoons cornflour

1 teaspoon caster sugar

sea salt and freshly ground black pepper

1 Make the noodle pancake and put to one side.

2 Mix all the ingredients for the marinade in a bowl, then add the beef, stir well to coat the meat and leave in the fridge for 1 hour.

3 Heat a wok, add a little oil and lightly fry the beef until it changes colour but is not quite cooked. Remove from the wok and put to one side.

4 Heat a little more oil in the wok and stir-fry the broccoli stalks until cooked, then remove from the wok and put to one side.

5 Stir the peanut paste and garlic into the oil in the wok until well mixed, then add all the ingredients for the soup base and bring to the boil.

6 Return the beef and broccoli to the wok and stir to mix well, then cook until heated through.

7 Put the noodle pancake in a serving dish, pour over the beef mixture and serve.

Below *Boy, those noodles were long!*

Finally, in case you think I have forgotten, to end this noodle section, I offer you a deliciously light vegetable fried-noodle pancake!

Vegetable fried-noodle pancake

Wood ears are dried fungus and are available in any Chinese supermarket. Before using, they should be soaked in a little warm water for about 20 minutes, then drained and patted dry.

500 g / 1 lb 2 oz noodle pancake (see
   page 147)
black bean paste
wine or rice vinegar
vegetable oil, for stir-frying

for the topping
20 g / ¾ oz Chinese dried black
   mushrooms, reconstituted in a little
   warm water for 30 minutes, stalks
   discarded, then drained and sliced
60 g / 2½ oz black wood ear,
   reconstituted in a little warm water for
   20 minutes, then chopped
150 g / 5 oz chopped choi sum cabbage,
   or stems of bok choi
1 medium carrot, peeled and cut into
   very thin strips
50 g / 2 oz bamboo shoots, finely sliced
100 g / 3½ oz fresh beansprouts
4 spring onions, trimmed and sliced
   diagonally into 2.5 cm / 1 inch lengths

for the soup base
675 ml / 1 pint 3 fl oz vegetable stock
2 tablespoons light soy sauce
1 tablespoon oyster sauce
2 teaspoons cornflour
1 teaspoon caster sugar
a pinch of sea salt

1 Make the noodle pancake and put to one side.

2 Heat a wok, add some oil and stir-fry the sliced mushrooms and wood ear for 2–3 minutes, then add all the remaining topping ingredients and stir-fry for a couple of minutes until they have all softened.

3 Mix the ingredients for the soup base in a bowl, then add to the wok and bring to the boil.

4 Place the noodle pancake in a serving dish and pour over the vegetable mixture.

5 Mix some black bean paste with enough vinegar to loosen it and serve separately in a small bowl.

Right *Bok choi for sale in a street market.*

Rice

Now to the vexed subject of rice, which is, of course, virtually the staple diet of China. The dishes I have selected for this book, in my view, either do not need rice at all, or if they do, it should be simply boiled, or better still, cooked in an electric rice cooker, which keeps the rice warm over two or three hours, as that is how long my feasts take to eat.

You can, of course, flavour the rice with a little saffron, or indeed you can cook it and leave it to go cold and then stir-fry it in vegetable oil or a little sesame oil and add into it, for example, cooked peas, small shrimps or prawns, little pieces of chicken or roasted Chinese pork, and maybe a chilli or two if you wish. One of the popular but very simple rice dishes is to take cold cooked rice, stir-fry it and stir in a couple of beaten whole eggs. Again you may wish to add some peas or shrimps. Or you can cook my Luxury fried rice below.

If you are using a rice cooker, just follow the instructions on the cooker. The ratio of 1 cup rice to 2 cups water is the same as if you boiled it in a pan.

Luxury fried rice

250 g/9 oz long-grain rice

3 eggs

3 or 4 Chinese dried black mushrooms, reconstituted in a little warm water for 30 minutes, stalks discarded, then drained and chopped

4 or 5 spring onions, trimmed and finely chopped (use the white and the green)

100 g/3½ oz shelled small raw prawns

50 g/2 oz cooked pork or chicken, or a mixture of both, diced

50 g/2 oz fresh bamboo shoots, parboiled in boiling salted water for 5 minutes, then drained and chopped

25 g/1 oz defrosted frozen peas

light soy sauce

sea salt and freshly ground black pepper

vegetable oil, for stir-frying

1 Wash and drain the rice and cook in your newly acquired electric rice cooker.

2 While this is cooking, beat the eggs with a little water, salt and pepper, then make a fairly firm, flat omelette. Once cooked, put to one side and allow to cool, Once the omelette is cold, cut it into small pieces.

3 When the rice is cooked, spread it thinly on a shallow tray and leave to cool (if you leave it in a mountain it will carry on cooking – not desirable!).

4 Heat a wok, add a little oil and stir-fry the mushrooms and spring onions for 2–3 minutes.

5 Add all the remaining ingredients except the omelette and soy sauce and stir-fry for a minute or so, then add the rice and continue to stir-fry until the rice has taken a little colour.

6 Add a few dashes of soy sauce, mix well and, finally, stir in the omelette pieces.

Right *Plain boiled rice.*

Vegetables

扁豆
18元1斤
3.5元2斤

Above left to right *Mrs Li cleans herbs found in the mountains around the Great Wall; imaginatively carved vegetables; a vendor arranges many different vegetables in a street market.* Opposite *Chinese cabbage.*

Vegetables

Chinese cuisine has an enormous variety of vegetables and, for the most part, they are cooked very simply – steamed, fried, braised or stir-fried, and for just a short time. They are rarely eaten raw.

If you are obliged to use canned vegetables, such as bamboo shoots, water chestnuts, etc., be sure you rinse them well and dry before use. Where you are using fresh vegetables, you can cut them into pretty shapes such as diamonds, julienne, flower shapes, etc.

Above *A visit to a Chinese street market will show you just how great a range of vegetables, particularly greens, you have to choose from.*

Fried greens with bean curd

1 block of bean curd, cut into strips

2 garlic cloves, peeled and finely
    chopped

250 g / 9 oz green vegetables, such as
    baby spinach leaves, chopped
    asparagus, broccoli florets, etc.

1 carrot, peeled and cut into very fine
    strips

a dash of soy sauce

sea salt, to taste

vegetable oil, for stir-frying

1 Heat a wok, add a little oil and fry the bean curd until golden on each side.

2 Add the garlic and stir-fry until the garlic has just taken on some colour.

3 Add your preferred greens and the carrot strips and stir-fry until just cooked. Season with soy sauce and salt and serve hot.

Mustard greens with oyster sauce

400 g / 14 oz mustard greens, cut into
    5 cm / 2 inch pieces
4 or 5 spring onions, trimmed and sliced
    diagonally into 5 cm / 2 inch lengths
2 tablespoons oyster sauce
2 tablespoons soy sauce
375 ml / 17 fl oz chicken or vegetable stock
½ teaspoon caster sugar
130 g can bamboo shoots, rinsed and dried
75 g / 3 oz sliced mushrooms (oyster, button
    or similar)
75 g / 3 oz straw mushrooms, or Chinese
    dried black mushrooms, reconstituted in
    a little warm water for 30 minutes, stalks
    discarded, then chopped
2 teaspoons cornflour mixed with a little cold
    water to the consistency of single cream
sea salt
vegetable oil, for frying

1 Bring a large pan of water to the boil, then blanch the mustard greens for about 1 minute. Plunge them into cold water to stop the cooking process, then drain.

2 Heat a wok, add a little oil and stir-fry the spring onions until just turning soft.

3 Add the oyster sauce, soy sauce, stock, sugar and a little salt to taste and bring to the boil, stirring all the time.

4 Add the remaining vegetables and the mustard greens, then stir in the cornflour mixture and cook, stirring, until the mixture has thickened. Serve hot.

Below *Note the sheer number of pots and pans.*

Green vegetables with oyster sauce and egg noodles

500 g / 1 lb 2 oz green vegetables, such
  as chopped purple sprouting broccoli,
  asparagus, baby spinach leaves, etc.
about 4 tablespoons vegetable or chicken
  stock
3 tablespoons vegetable oil
3 tablespoons oyster sauce
1 teaspoon sesame oil
1 teaspoon caster sugar
2 teaspoons cornflour mixed with a little
  cold water to the consistency of single
  cream
800 g / 1 lb 12 oz egg noodles
sea salt, to taste

1 Bring a large pan of salted water to the boil, add the vegetables and boil until just cooked, then drain and put to one side.

2 Add the stock, vegetable oil, oyster sauce, sesame oil, sugar and salt to the pan and bring to the boil, then add the vegetables. Stir in the cornflour mixture and cook, stirring, until the mixture has thickened.

3 Cook the noodles according to the instructions on the packet, drain and place in a serving dish.

4 Pour the vegetable mixture over the noodles and serve.

Fried tomatoes with egg

4 eggs, beaten
2 or 3 spring onions, trimmed and
  chopped
2 or 3 tomatoes, skinned and deseeded,
  then cut into quarters
1 tablespoon tomato ketchup
1 teaspoon caster sugar
sea salt, to taste
a little vegetable oil
a pinch of five-spice powder (see
  page 178), to finish
freshly chopped coriander leaves or
  parsley, to garnish

1 Heat a wok, add a little oil, then pour in the beaten eggs and cook until beginning to thicken.

2 Add the spring onions, tomatoes, ketchup, sugar and salt and continue cooking for 2–3 minutes until the egg has set.

3 Sprinkle on the five-spice powder and serve hot garnished with coriander or parsley.

Opposite Pile 'em high and sell 'em cheap. No 'hands-off' policy here.

An assortment of simmered vegetables

an assortment of your preferred
vegetables – about a handful of each,
such as cauliflower, baby sweetcorn,
broccoli, carrot, pepper, etc., cut into
attractively shaped pieces of equal
size
150 ml / 5 fl oz chicken or vegetable
stock
2 teaspoons cornflour mixed with a little
cold water to the consistency of single
cream
thick soy sauce
sea salt, to taste
vegetable oil, for stir-frying

1 Bring a large pan of water to the boil, then blanch all
the vegetables for about 30 seconds. Drain and put to
one side.

2 Heat a wok, add a little oil and stir-fry the drained
vegetables for 2–3 minutes.

3 Add the stock, cornflour mixture, soy sauce and
salt and continue to stir-fry until the sauce thickens,
then serve.

Below *Baby sweetcorn.*

Above *Cutting and cleaning mushrooms in Beihai Park.*

Mushrooms and pickled cabbage

2 tablespoons sea salt, plus a pinch

1 small white cabbage, cut into chunks, stalk discarded

5 or 6 large flat field mushrooms, cut into large chunky strips

4 Chinese dried black mushrooms, reconstituted in a little warm water for 30 minutes, stalks discarded, then cut into strips

2 tablespoons oyster sauce

1 teaspoon caster sugar

1 tablespoon cornflour mixed with a little cold water to the consistency of single cream

1 teaspoon sesame oil, for sprinkling

vegetable oil

1 Bring a large pan of water to the boil, then add the 2 tablespoons salt and a few drops of vegetable oil and blanch the cabbage for about 1 minute. Drain and put to one side.

2 Heat a wok, add a little vegetable oil and stir-fry all the mushrooms until they are soft and giving off a little liquid.

3 Add the oyster sauce, sugar and a pinch of salt and continue to stir-fry for another 30 seconds, then add the cornflour mixture and stir until the sauce thickens.

4 Sprinkle the mushrooms with the sesame oil and serve on a dish surrounded by the cabbage.

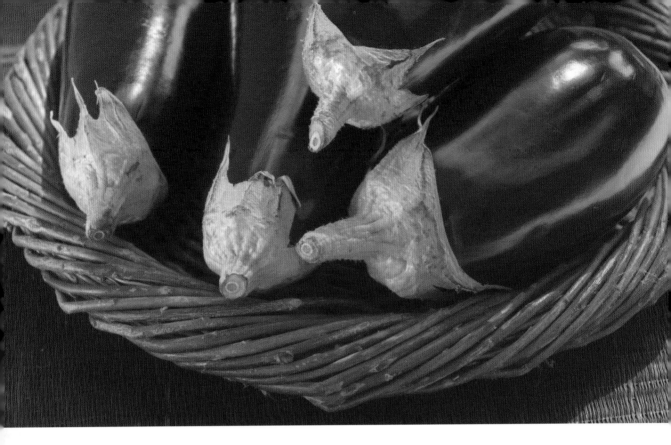

Fried aubergines

2 large aubergines, trimmed and cut into
  2.5 cm / 1 inch cubes
2 large flat field mushrooms, sliced, or
  5 Chinese dried black mushrooms,
  reconstituted in a little warm water for
  30 minutes, stalks discarded, then
  sliced
1 red chilli, deseeded and finely chopped
1 teaspoon sea salt
1 tablespoon chilli sauce
2 teaspoons cornflour mixed with a little
  cold water to the consistency of single
  cream
vegetable oil, for stir-frying
a few drops of sesame oil and a pinch
  of five-spice powder (see page 178),
  to finish
1 bunch of parsley, finely chopped,
  to garnish

1 Heat a wok, add a little vegetable oil and quickly stir-fry the aubergines until tender, then remove with a slotted spoon and drain on kitchen paper. Discard the oil and wipe out the wok.

2 Heat some more oil in the wok, add the mushrooms and stir-fry for about 30 seconds, then add the chopped chilli and stir-fry for another 30 seconds.

3 Add the aubergine cubes, the salt, chilli sauce and cornflour mixture and stir-fry until the mixture thickens.

4 Turn out into a serving dish, sprinkle on a few drops of sesame oil and a pinch of five-spice powder, and serve garnished with the chopped parsley.

Curried mushrooms

200 g / 7 oz peas
2.5 cm / 1 inch piece fresh root ginger,
    peeled and finely sliced
200 g / 7 oz button mushrooms, sliced in
    half or quarters depending on the size
3 baby sweetcorn, cut into 1 cm / ½ inch
    pieces
2.5 cm / 1 inch piece carrot, peeled and
    finely cubed
3 teaspoons cornflour mixed with a little
    cold water to the consistency of single
    cream
2 tablespoons mild curry powder
sea salt, to taste
vegetable oil, for frying
a few drops of sesame oil, to finish
a handful of freshly chopped parsley or
    coriander leaves, to garnish

1 Bring a pan of water to the boil, then plunge the peas in and blanch for about 2 minutes. Drain and put to one side.

2 Heat a wok, add a little vegetable oil and stir-fry the ginger, mushrooms, sweetcorn, carrot and peas for 2–3 minutes.

3 Add the cornflour mixture and curry powder and stir until thickened – add some more water if the mixture is dry, then season to taste.

4 Cook for a further minute or so, then pour into a serving dish and sprinkle over a few drops of sesame oil. Serve garnished with the chopped parsley or coriander.

Stir-fried mixed mushrooms

Get a selection of dried Chinese mushrooms and cloud ears fungus, reconstitute them in a little warm water for 30 minutes, discard the stalks, then dry them. Get an equal quantity of mixed fresh mushrooms. Heat a wok, add a little vegetable oil and stir-fry all the mushrooms for 2–3 minutes.

Sprinkle in some finely chopped spring onions, some soy sauce, a pinch of five-spice powder (see page 178) and salt and pepper to taste and toss to warm through, then serve.

Stir-fried peppers

Take 1 red pepper and 1 green pepper, cut them in half, deseed them and remove the pith, then cut them into nice shapes. Peel 1 onion and cut into 2.5 cm / 1 inch chunks. Take a 2.5 cm / 1 inch piece fresh root ginger, peel it and cut into fine julienne strips. Peel a couple of garlic cloves and chop finely.

Heat a wok, add some vegetable oil and stir-fry all the above for 2–3 minutes, so that they are still slightly crunchy, then serve with either oyster sauce or black bean sauce.

Mixed vegetables with lotus root

1 lotus root (or if unavailable, 1 can lotus root), peeled and sliced

4 or 5 Chinese dried black mushrooms, reconstituted in a little warm water for 30 minutes, stalks discarded, then sliced

½ carrot, peeled and cut into strips

1 head of broccoli, cut into chunks

100 g / 3½ oz stringed mangetout

2.5 cm / 1 inch piece fresh root ginger, peeled and finely sliced

1 tablespoon oyster sauce

1 tablespoon soy sauce

1 tablespoon white rice vinegar

a splash of rice wine, sake or dry sherry

1 teaspoon caster sugar

1 teaspoon sea salt

2 teaspoons cornflour mixed with a little cold water to the consistency of single cream

vegetable oil, for stir-frying

a few drops of sesame oil, to finish

1 Bring a large pan of water to the boil, then blanch the lotus root, mushrooms, carrot, broccoli and mangetout for about 1 minute. Drain and put to one side.

2 Heat a wok, add a little vegetable oil and stir-fry the vegetables and ginger for a minute or so, then add the oyster sauce, soy sauce, vinegar, rice wine, sake or sherry, the sugar and salt and stir well.

3 Add the cornflour mixture and cook, stirring, until the mixture thickens a little.

4 Tip into a serving dish, sprinkle over a little sesame oil and serve.

Right *I love the Chinese markets.*
Opposite *Lotus root.*

Fried mushrooms with chilli

2 tablespoons cornflour

2 egg whites

8 large flat field mushrooms, stalks
    discarded, then thickly sliced

1 heaped teaspoon dried chilli flakes

sweet chilli sauce

vegetable oil, for deep-frying

1 Whip together the cornflour with the egg whites to
make a batter.

2 Heat sufficient oil for deep-frying in a pan to about
180°C/350°F.

3 Dip the mushroom slices into the batter until they are
well coated, then drop into the hot oil – do not crowd the
pan, cook about 4 at a time – and cook until they have
risen to the surface and are golden.

4 Remove each batch with a slotted spoon, drain on
kitchen paper and keep warm while you cook the
remaining mushrooms.

5 Transfer to a serving platter, sprinkle on the chilli flakes
and serve hot with a dipping bowl of chilli sauce.

And then, of course, there are the three famous Chinese greens:

The choi sum, a.k.a. Chinese flowering cabbage

The bok or pak choi

The nappa cabbage, a.k.a. pale Chinese leaves, celery cabbage, Peking cabbage
(the other two, above, have dark leaves and crunchy white stems)

All the above can be simply steamed and served with
oyster sauce, or quickly blanched in vegetable or chicken
stock, drained and then stir-fried in vegetable oil and
again served with oyster sauce. Simple, delicious and
incredibly healthy!

Opposite Steamed bok choi.

Dips, Sauces and Accompaniments

Above left to right *Jasmine tea; pickled ginger; a fabulous array of spices at Chaoyang wholesale market.*

Dips, Sauces and Accompaniments

Many Chinese dishes are accompanied by little bowls of extras – whether just a simple dish of vinegar in which to dunk your dumplings, or an eye-watering chilli dipping sauce. They add that little bit of 'umph' to the food and it's always worth trying them when offered.

You can eat pickled ginger as a nibble, in stir-frys or as a garnish. It has a very refreshing flavour, is easy to make and will keep for ages in the fridge. Fried garlic or onion flakes are also good as garnishes – quick and simple to make.

Five-spice powder is used not only in marinades but also as an integral part of many dishes and it adds a distinctive flavour to whatever it's cooked with. Make up a batch and it will keep for ages. Then there's chilli oil – a basic ingredient of all the hot sauces. Make it as hot as you like!

Offer dips and sauces in small bowls for diners to help themselves to.

Below *Many of the roots, spices, leaves and herbs are used in Chinese medicine.*

Five-spice powder

1 cinnamon stick, about 10 cm / 4 inches
   in length, broken into 4 pieces
100 Chinese or Sichuan peppercorns
2 teaspoons dried fennel seeds
15 whole cloves
4 whole star anise

1 Tip all the ingredients into a coffee grinder and grind to a fine powder.

2 Store in a jar with an airtight lid for up to 3 months.

Chilli oil

75 ml / 3 fl oz vegetable oil
75 ml / 3 fl oz sesame oil
2½ tablespoons dried chilli flakes

1 Heat the vegetable and sesame oils to smoking point in a small pan, then turn off the heat immediately.

2 Allow the oil to cool a little, then stir in the chilli flakes.

3 Transfer the chilli oil to a jar (something like a kilner jar), cover and leave to infuse for 3–4 days.

4 Strain through a fine sieve into an attractive serving bottle. This will keep for 3 months in the fridge.

Ginger sauce

1 jar sweet pickled ginger, strained and minced

4 Chinese dried black mushrooms, reconstituted in a little warm water for 30 minutes, stalks discarded, then finely chopped

2 or 3 spring onions, trimmed and very finely chopped

2 or 3 red chillies, very finely chopped (deseeded if you like)

a couple of dashes of light soy sauce

120 ml/4 fl oz white rice vinegar

100 g/3½ oz caster sugar

175 ml/6 fl oz water

1 teaspoon cornflour mixed with a little cold water to the consistency of single cream

1 Put all the ingredients except the cornflour in a stainless steel saucepan (don't use an aluminium pan) and simmer for about 5 minutes.

2 Add the cornflour mixture to the sauce and cook for a further minute, stirring until thickened. Use hot, or cool and pour into a jar, then seal and keep in the fridge for up to 2 weeks.

Chilli soy sauce

1 small bottle chilli sauce

an equal volume of light soy sauce

2 garlic cloves, peeled and very, very finely chopped, then crushed to a purée with the back of a tablespoon

2 thin slices peeled fresh root ginger, very finely chopped and then crushed as above

1 teaspoon caster sugar

2 teaspoons soft brown sugar

1 Combine all the ingredients in a bowl and stir until the sugar has dissolved.

2 Transfer to a jar or bottle, cover and leave to infuse for 1 day before using. Keep refrigerated and shake well before serving.

Garlic sauce

6 fat garlic cloves, peeled and finely
  chopped, then crushed to a purée
  with the back of a tablespoon
120 ml / 4 fl oz white rice vinegar or white
  wine vinegar
100 g / 3½ oz caster sugar
2 teaspoons chilli paste
250 ml / 8½ fl oz water
½ teaspoon sea salt

1 Place all the ingredients in a stainless-steel saucepan (don't use an aluminium pan) and bring to the boil.

2 Reduce the heat and simmer gently until the sauce is reduced by half and has thickened to the consistency of double cream. You can use this sauce immediately, hot, or it can be cooled and stored in a jar with an airtight lid in the fridge for 4–6 weeks and reheated as required.

Soy ginger dipping sauce

100 ml / 3½ fl oz light soy sauce
2.5 cm / 1 inch piece fresh root ginger,
  peeled and very finely chopped
sea salt and freshly ground black pepper
a dash of sesame oil

1 Combine all the ingredients in a small bowl and leave in the fridge for about 1 hour for the flavours to develop before using.

Ginger and spring onion sauce

This goes particularly well with crisply fried poultry or duck.

100 ml / 3½ fl oz vegetable oil
1 small piece fresh root ginger, peeled
  and very finely chopped, then crushed
  to a purée with the back of a
  tablespoon
5 spring onions, trimmed and very finely
  chopped
1 heaped teaspoon sea salt

1 Heat the oil in a saucepan until warm. Add all the remaining ingredients and cook gently for 2–3 minutes.

2 Serve in little bowls.

Above left to right *Dark soy sauce, light soy sauce.*

Sweet and sour sauce

100 ml / 3½ fl oz white rice vinegar or
white wine vinegar

1 tablespoon tomato ketchup

2 teaspoons dark soy sauce

4 tablespoons soft brown sugar

2 teaspoons cornflour mixed with a little
cold water to the consistency of single
cream

2 tablespoons tinned pineapple chunks,
drained and diced very small

1 Mix all the ingredients except the cornflour and
pineapple in a small stainless steel saucepan (don't use
an aluminium pan) and bring to the boil.

2 Remove from the heat and immediately pour in the
cornflour mixture to thicken, then add the pineapple.
This sauce can be used hot or cold.

Chilli dipping sauce

3 or 4 green chillies, sliced and deseeded
60 ml / 2½ fl oz white rice vinegar or
    white wine vinegar
2 teaspoons sea salt
2 teaspoons caster sugar

1 Combine all the ingredients in a bowl and leave to marinate in the fridge for about 3 hours before using.

Pickled ginger

1 medium-sized piece fresh root ginger,
    peeled and cut into razor-thin slivers
2 teaspoons caster sugar
white rice wine or white rice vinegar (if
    using rice vinegar, add another
    teaspoon of caster sugar)

1 Place the ginger and sugar in a jar and pour in sufficient vinegar or wine to just cover the ginger.

2 Seal the jar with an airtight lid, refrigerate and wait for the ginger to turn slightly pink before using – this will depend on the freshness of your ginger, but it's generally a few days.

Fried garlic flakes

These are wonderful sprinkled over all manner of Chinese dishes. You can do the same with peeled shallots. For garlic lovers, you can also serve them cold as a nibble.

10 fat garlic cloves, peeled and cut
    lengthways into very thin slices
vegetable oil, for frying

1 Heat the oil in a pan, add the garlic and fry until golden brown, but be careful not to burn them.

2 Lift out of the oil, drain on kitchen paper and serve hot.

Opposite left to right *Chilli dipping sauce, pickled ginger, fried garlic flakes.*

Chinese mixed pickles

for the pickles

3 large carrots, peeled

450 g / 1 lb white Chinese radish, peeled

1 cucumber, peeled, halved lengthways
and deseeded

4 stringed celery stalks

8 medium onions, peeled

1 large red pepper and 1 large green
pepper, each deseeded and pith
removed

2 litres / 3½ pints water

115 g / 4 oz peeled fresh root ginger,
finely sliced

for the pickling liquid

750 ml / 1¼ pints white rice vinegar or
white wine vinegar

375 ml / 13 fl oz water

750 g / 1 lb 10 oz caster sugar

1½ teaspoons coarse salt

1 Combine all the ingredients for the pickling liquid in a stainless steel saucepan (don't use an aluminium pan) and bring to the boil. Stir for a couple of minutes, then remove from the heat and leave to cool.

2 For the pickles, cut the carrots, radish and cucumber into thin strips about 5 cm / 2 inches long. Cut the celery into 1 cm / ½ inch diagonal slices. Cut the onions into 5 mm / ¼ inch diagonal slices. Cut the peppers into 1 cm / ½ inch cubes.

3 Bring the water to the boil in a large pan, then switch off the heat and plunge the vegetables and ginger into the water and leave for approximately 2 minutes.

4 Drain the vegetables in a colander, pat dry with kitchen paper and leave to cool.

5 Once cold, pack the vegetables into jars and pour over the pickling liquid, making sure the vegetables are completely covered.

6 Seal the jars with airtight lids and store in the fridge for at least 1 week before serving.

Right Pickles are eaten for breakfast in Northern China. Opposite Many varieties of pickles for sale in a market outside the White Cloud Taoist Temple in Beijing.

To finish your meal

Despite the toffee apples and toffee bananas that invariably end Chinese meals in this country, in China family meals usually end with fresh fruit and tea. That's not to say the Chinese don't like sweet things – steamed sweet buns, sweet rice dishes, custards and dumplings are popular to snack on during the day and are widely available as street food.

However, at formal dinners or banquets, sweet dishes are frequently served between courses in the same way as sorbets are used in the West, and on these occasions sweet soups are popular.

The sub-tropical areas of China provide a large variety of luscious fruit – pineapples, mangoes, lychees, star fruit and oranges, to name a few. For special occasions, various fruits will be prepared and offered in hollowed-out melons – an attractive way of serving fruit. Or you could use a pineapple in the same way.

Oranges, along with a final pot of tea, are traditionally offered at the end of a meal in restaurants – sweet and juicy, they refresh and cleanse the palate after the many courses that have gone before.

And then, of course, you may even be offered a fortune cookie – crack it open, unfold the prediction, and your fortune will appear. Hey ho!

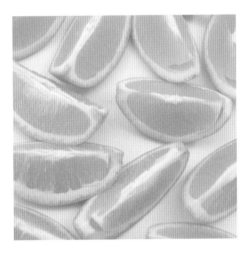

Index